THE STRATEGY NOTE

Cultivate the Leadership Discipline
of the Strategy Note

JOHN HALE

www.halecg.com

Copyright © 2022 by John Hale. All rights reserved.

Published by Hale Consulting Group
267 Grey Street
South Brisbane 4101 Australia
www.halecg.com

This book or any portion thereof may not be reproduced or used in any manner whatsoever without the express written approval of the author.

Limit of Liability/Disclaimer of Warranty: While the publisher and author have used their best efforts in preparing this book, they make no warranties regarding the accuracy or completeness of the contents of this book. They expressly disclaim any implied warranties of merchantability or fitness for a particular purpose. No warranty may be offered by sales representatives or written sales materials. The publisher and author are not acting as advisors in this book.

This book and the content provided herein are simply for educational purposes and do not in any way take the place of business advice from a professional advisor, be that strategic, financial, legal or otherwise. The information and strategies contained herein may not be suitable for your situation. This book includes non-factual models and metaphors from the author's life and narratives and ideas adapted from many sources. All effort has been made to ensure that the content provided in this book is inspiring and helpful for readers. However, this book is not an exhaustive treatment of the subjects contained within it. The author assumes no liability for losses or damages due to the information provided. You are responsible for your own choices, actions, and results.

Illustrations: Lauren Hale
Book Design: Jana Rade

SECOND EDITION
Paperback: ISBN 978-0-6486590-2-0
Ebook: ISBN 978-0-6486590-3-7

A catalogue record for this book is available from the National Library of Australia

By her example, Jan Hale, my mother, showed me our precious connection to the natural world and how to align right understanding with right action.

This book is dedicated to her.

CONTENTS

INTRODUCTION
THE STRATEGY NOTE	5
A FORMULA FOR SUCCESS	9
THE BUS	12

TASK ONE – WRITE YOUR RECOMMENDATION
LESSONS FROM CORONAVIRUS	18
TAKING CHARGE	19
INTUITION	21

TASK TWO – REPORT YOUR HEALTH
FINANCIAL RATIOS	34
LEADERSHIP SCORE	37
TRIBE SCORE	39

TASK THREE – SUMMARIZE YOUR ANALYSIS
WIDE ANGLE LENS	52
SELL THE MILLS	54
YOUR ANALYSIS	55

TASK FOUR – NAME YOUR OPTIONS
LIFESAVING	66
FUTURE OPTIONS	69
DECISION TOOLS	70

TASK FIVE – GROW DIGITAL WINGS

LIFE AND DEATH	80
DIGITAL WINGS	81
STAGES OF BUSINESS GROWTH	85

TASK SIX – ALIGN YOUR ACTIONS

UNITED BREAKS GUITARS	99
CLAIM TO FAME	101
NEXT STEPS	102

CONCLUSION

'UBER IT'	113
END GAMES	114
GAME ON	116

EPILOGUE - THE NEXT LEVEL

EXISTENTIAL FLEXIBILITY	119
PLAY A BIGGER GAME	123
CREATE YOUR FLYWHEEL	129

APPENDICES

INDUSTRY ATTRACTIVENESS	135
CLAIM TO FAME	143
CRITICAL SUCCESS FACTORS	149
CUSTOMER INTIMACY WHEEL	155
SCENARIO PLANNING	161
DECISION TREES	169
EXPECTED MONETARY VALUES	177

ENDNOTES	187
ACKNOWLEDGEMENTS	193
ABOUT THE AUTHOR	195

INTRODUCTION

Global leadership is in crisis.

It is difficult to find examples of good leadership anywhere.

From a laundry list which includes Boris Johnson, Donald Trump, Benjamin Netanyahu, Vladimir Putin, and Xi Jinping, one might mistake incompetence, bribery, corruption, embezzlement, ethnic cleansing and genocide as valid strategies for top leaders.

Oligarchic business leaders like Amazon's Bezos and Facebook's Zuckerberg, simply offer unpalatable examples. Despite his immense wealth, Bezos lacks the philanthropic generosity shared by many who give generously despite having very little. Zuckerberg has us addicted to two and a half hours of social media per day and repeatedly violates our trust and privacy in his pursuit of profit.

Young Swedish environmental activist, Greta Thunberg's 2019 address to the United Nations could well have been addressed to business leaders:

THE STRATEGY NOTE

> "You have stolen my dreams and my childhood with your empty words. And yet I'm one of the lucky ones. People are suffering. People are dying. Entire ecosystems are collapsing. We are at the beginning of a mass extinction, and all you can talk about is money and fairy tales of eternal economic growth. How dare you!"

As one of the world's youngest and well-informed leaders, Greta has a strategy for saving the planet. During 2016, she analysed emissions by country and activity. Greta knows that a flight from Stockholm to Rome pollutes the atmosphere with 2.7 tonnes of CO_2 and 3.4 tonnes of even more damaging non-CO_2 gases. Since then, Greta, her family and many others no longer fly, to help save the planet. Greta and hundreds of millions of outraged people regularly protest for climate change and the rights of minorities. In time, they may dethrone today's toxic leaders and help our planet recover.

As a business leader, you can also play your part.

Greta Thunberg, who was not even born in the year 2000, might have been helpful to Selene, an idealistic but disillusioned business leader.

In 2000, as I listened to Selene, she described her despair.

"Screw it. Nothing works."

"No one will buy my idea. Nobody cares for this toxic planet."

INTRODUCTION

It was an unusually hot day for October. Ten minutes earlier, I had been drinking coffee in Bob's office. Bob, an accountant, wanted me to meet another of his troubled clients.

A yellow cab pulled up. Selene stepped out.

From the window, I saw Selene approaching. She was thin and pale, with dark windswept hair. Upon entering the office, Selene seemed agitated.

Bob spoke nervously, "Selene, meet John; maybe John can help."

Selene groaned, "I doubt it."

My eyes widened. I let Selene's remark dissolve on my next exhale.

Selene, a failed business leader, was burdened by debt and a custody battle.

As Selene felt safer, her eyes released tears.

The antique clock in Bob's office chimed. Selene pulled herself together. I sensed from Bob that this assignment would be pro bono. Bob knew me well. In do or die situations, I make sure businesses do. Bob smiled at me. I smiled back.

I said to myself, 'Game on.'

THE STRATEGY NOTE

I encouraged Selene, "If I could grant you anything you want, what would it be?"

The blood returned to Selene's face. Selene revealed her business idea. She wanted to formulate, make and sell a range of all-natural, environmentally friendly and allergy-proof personal care products.

To grow her business, Selene needed real courage. She also needed a plan.

Two days later, I sent Selene a one-page strategy note. My note gave her an action plan she could draw from moving forward. I was unsure whether she could avoid bankruptcy. Nevertheless, Selene now had a strategy note. A single page containing a pragmatic assessment, an overview of options, a recommendation for growing her business and three action steps.

Five years later, Selene contacted me. I was curious to hear how she was doing. Had she found the courage to grow her business? I wanted to understand if the strategy note had helped. Selene testified that the strategy note gave her business clear options. These options were invaluable in leading her company to take brave decisions and actions. She revealed that her company was the leader in its field and had just won the state-wide business award as the best business in its category.

I then asked Selene, "How are you feeling?"

Selene replied, "People really do care about the planet and my ideas!"

INTRODUCTION

I winked at Selene, "Nothing works."

Selene laughed, "True. But your strategy note did."

THE STRATEGY NOTE

Economists say the pandemic and increasing climate change created 'the perfect storm' for businesses worldwide. The challenge for business leaders is to find ways to re-build their businesses in sustainable ways and improve their leadership effectiveness. As a leader, you can do both by cultivating the discipline of The Strategy Note. The process is laid out in this book in a conversational and interactive style. This book offers you just as many questions as answers. I invite you to write in the book and make notes as you learn how to construct a one-page strategy note.

The crowning aspect of leadership is to align people with strategy in ways that do not harm the planet. The Strategy Note can assist a leader to do both. A strategy note is a time-limited one-pager that sheds light on strategy and communicates the actions needed.

The most effective strategic plans do not contain fifty pages of analysis and industry references, which no board member, manager or employee wants to read. Strategy and recommendations are best understood in person. When a leader cannot share recommendations in person, they must use another form of communication.

THE STRATEGY NOTE

To be an effective leader, you must create a regular script to be shared in people's presence and absence. This script is best communicated on a single page and, in a format that reliably informs the reader of the strategic intent and the actions needed. As your business strategy and tactics change, your script needs to change. Each updated version needs to be short, efficient and effective. Your script is not a strategic plan, but rather a note which keeps delivering on your strategic planning process. A strategy note is a brief note that strikes a chord with each of its readers. The Strategy Note is a powerful tool for aligning the actions of your people with your strategy.

Even at a low point, Selene was still a visionary leader. I valued Selene's approach. She linked right understanding, right relationship and right action[1]. She understood the damaging impact of chemical compounds in regular consumer soaps, shampoos and cleansing agents. This understanding helped Selene consider the ways products can have healthier relationships with consumers and the environment. She then acted to create something new, valuable and unique. We can apply right understanding, right relationship and right action in two ways. Firstly, rationally and secondly, ethically. From a rational and practical viewpoint, as your understanding of events in your business changes, your stakeholder relationships change, and your actions should shift in turn.

From an ethical viewpoint, your understanding of the morally right path for your business helps you to make the right choices. These choices include choosing business relationships with people of honor and acting in ways that are beneficial, legal and ethical. It may be economically rational to farm and slaughter large animals, create

INTRODUCTION

wet food markets and drive petrol cars. However, these activities increase global warming, spawn pandemics and increase the risk of morbidities such as lung cancer, heart attacks and stroke.

Thankfully, more businesses are allowing ethics to shape their understanding, relationship choices and activities in ways that have a positive impact on society and the natural world. Companies with a social and environmental purpose energize employees[2]. Having ethical principles and a proper strategic planning process are foundational leadership qualities. However, this does not guarantee success. Alas, I have seen many ethical businesses whose strategy fails to reach its target. Often, when the rubber hits the road, it can be hard to find evidence of an intentional plan anywhere. Intentional plans are needed, and they should be replaced with updated versions, each time the business priorities change. It is for this reason I created The Strategy Note.

THE STRATEGY NOTE

STRATEGY NOTE — JUNE QUARTER

1. RECOMMENDATION

2. DEBT SCORE   QUICK SCORE   LEADER SCORE   TRIBE SCORE

3. ANALYSIS

4. OPTIONS

5. DIGITAL WINGS

6. NEXT STEPS

INTRODUCTION

To create strategy notes for your business, you only need to carry out six tasks.

> Task 1. Write Your Recommendation
> Task 2. Report Your Health
> Task 3. Summarize Your Analysis
> Task 4 Name Your Options
> Task 5. Grow Digital Wings
> Task 6. Align Your Actions

These six tasks produce an ongoing one-page communique that helps your team remember the agreed strategy and align their future actions with it.

A FORMULA FOR SUCCESS

With a grateful heart, I remember Bill[3]. Bill was one of my heroes. He was my former professor and a good friend. He taught me many things about business and life. It was Bill who first introduced me to the idea of a strategy note. Bill also introduced me to legendary business leader, TJ Rogers, who I will introduce to you in the next chapter.

I was sad when Bill passed away in 2019.

Bill's passing reminded me of my own mortality. No individual or business lasts forever. When visiting Bill in Los Angeles, Bill and I would head for the beachfront down Ocean Park Boulevard. We'd joke, talk philosophically and share inspirational stories of human grit in times of adversity. He was always humble. Bill was a pragmatic optimist who embodied a healthy mixture of passion, purpose and humor.

Bill used to say, "When the going gets tough, my recommendation is to get going!"

I used to retort, "When the going gets tough, get smarter."

We smiled to show each other we were both right.

Sometimes success means showing up. Often success is about falling ninety-nine times and getting up a hundred or simply hanging in there after others have let go.

Bill often joked, "Sometimes, you don't have to outrun a hungry lion. Success can be as easy as outrunning the next guy!"

In the last lecture of Bill's entrepreneurship courses, he would share the following success relationship with his students.

SUCCESS = TALENT + PREPARATION + TIMING

The best leaders ensure they have a talented team that prepares a future course for the business. The timing of key moves, like which market to enter, when to switch distributors, change suppliers, or exit the industry, are also important.

INTRODUCTION

After a few moments, once students had made a note of the formula, Bill's eyes would twinkle and he'd say, "And of course, a bit of luck always helps!"

But how important is luck?

What was that lucky twinkle in Bill's wise eyes saying?

A year before I met Bill, he had been awarded the Citibank Prize for Excellence in Teaching for the seventh time. A Business Week survey named him one of the Best Professors of Entrepreneurship in America. This did not surprise me. Bill has been one of the best teachers I have come across. As a highly accomplished teacher, Bill reminded me of famous golfer Arnold Palmer.

Arnold once said, "The more I practice, the luckier I get."

And as a golfer, having added ninety-five professional wins to his name, Arnold should know.

So, I have added to Bill's formula.

SUCCESS = TALENT + PREPARATION + TIMING + **PRACTICE**

A talented business that considers its strategy infrequently and implements only a few recommendations will encounter problems. This type of business lacks practice and skill in formulating and implementing strategic recommendations. On the other hand, a leader or business owner who regularly practices the art of making recommendations using a one-page strategy note becomes a master at strategic execution. Firms that become skilled at moral guidance, strategic dialogue and the execution of bold recommendations are unlikely to run out of luck. They make their luck through practice.

THE BUS

Author Jim Collins has taught leaders worldwide the understanding that getting the right people in the right seats helps ensure the right actions happen. Jim believes that getting the right people on the bus and in the right seats should occur before having any conversation about strategy[4]. Indeed, in my discussions with venture capitalists and astute early-stage investors, I would echo the same sentiments as Jim. The business idea is less important than the quality of the team assembled to deliver on it.

Having worked with many start-ups and dozens of larger firms, I have witnessed brilliant business opportunities destroyed by having the wrong people on the bus or placed in the wrong seats. I have also seen some marginal business ideas do well by having an excellent team in place. The marginalization of Nokia and the rise of Apple highlight this. In 2007, the Nokia Board was very much a homogenous 'boys club' comprising men of similar ages, who all attended similar private schools and universities in Finland. At Apple, the diversity policy encouraged leadership recruitment from around the world. Apple was talented, highly organized and disciplined. When asked about his hiring policy, Steve Jobs shared that he liked to hire the smartest people, regardless of race, gender or nationality[5].

'Why so, Steve?'

'So, they can tell me what to do.'

Can a business with a bus full of talented people, who regularly formulate and implement strategy, still fail? Yes, it can. Especially, if those people are unethical. Failed firms like Enron and Arthur Anderson had skilled and strategically adept top leadership teams, with weak moral compasses. If you are happy with the tribe on your bus, that's great news. If not, get talented and ethical people on the bus, and as kindly and intelligently as possible, get the wrong people off it.

It is vital to choose mentors, teachers, leaders, colleagues and employees carefully. Over time, we gradually become like the people around us. For nearly a decade, Uber reportedly had a culture of unethical leadership and a discriminatory workplace[6]. There was a tight inner circle of executives, for whom unethical behavior appeared to have no consequences. In recent years, Uber has worked hard to get the right people on the bus.

It was an honor to share part of my 'bus ride' with Bill and by association with TJ Rogers. In my strategy note to Selene, I recommended that she take a 'bus ride' with Andrew, who could help her with funding, product development and distribution. Andrew was a seasoned market player who was looking for partners like Selene. Do you have the right people on your bus? Is it time to dismiss the wrong people and find the right ones? When the right people are in the right seats, make sure you have a shared and ethical process for regular strategy formulation and review. Once you have an agreed recommendation, it's time to share it by writing a one-page strategy note.

TASK ONE

WRITE YOUR RECOMMENDATION

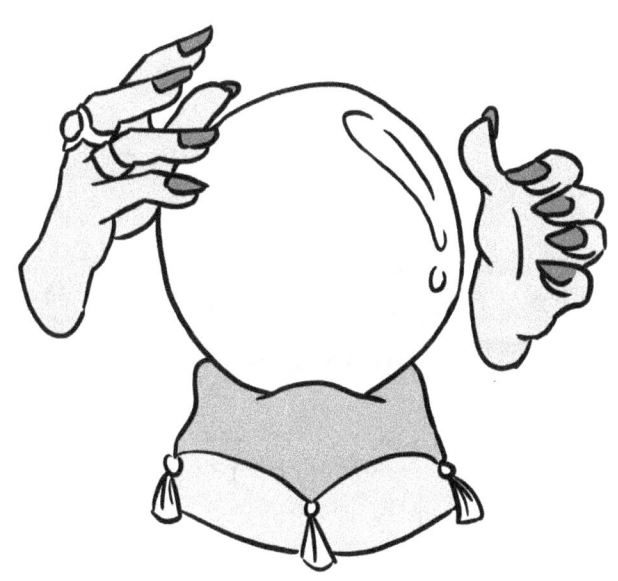

THE STRATEGY NOTE

TASK ONE
WRITE YOUR RECOMMENDATION

Once the dry, dusty air from the car park settled, I spotted him. It was Paul, another of Bob's clients. I noted as I walked towards the factory that Paul seemed dangerously overweight.

Paul kindly finished his cigarette before greeting me.

Then together, we entered the admin building. Once in the office, Paul complained that he worked seventy hours per week. His business employed sixty people, and they generated twenty-million dollars of sales per year. Yet net profits were just one percent of sales. Clearly something was wrong.

I worked alongside Paul for four weeks and found his workers were gaming the incentive systems and hurting production. We improved the business by creating new rules that empowered his people and helped them lead one another. Paul learned to work on the business, instead of being the 'fire-fighter' who solved every small problem.

Paul used to say, "I am solving another problem right now, but wait there and don't do anything. I'll come down to your area and solve your team's problems in about forty minutes."

Paul let his people keep him dancing from dawn until dusk.

TASK ONE: WRITE YOUR RECOMMENDATION

Eventually, Paul sat behind his desk and said to his supervisors, "Bring me solutions, not problems."

Paul's supervisors learned to say the same thing to workers. Net profits rose to twelve percent.

At the end of the assignment Paul said to me, "You've fixed my business. I would never have predicted this."

If you could look into your crystal ball, what would you see? For most of us, when it is all said and done, predicting the future is impossible.

Nevertheless, you can create your future.

When Bill introduced me to TJ Rogers, by handing me a note entitled No Excuses Management by TJ Rogers[7], I would never have predicted that it would plant a seed which would transform my work with clients. However, I suspect Bill did! I want to share the three lessons I took from TJ. These three lessons have helped me to support many businesses needing to make rewarding decisions, manage risk and create brighter futures.

Businesses that regularly make risky yet rewarding choices tend to create the brightest futures. As you will see, better results can come from having repeated up-to-date recommendations with action steps. I originally designed the one-page strategy note to help communicate recommendations to clients like Paul, Selene, and their key stakeholders. Successful leaders are always making recommendations around their approach to the future - a risky step at times. But not changing is also dangerous. The best recommendations take risks into account and provide appropriate action steps that drive the desired changes and offer valuable lessons.

The first lesson I took from TJ is that strategic plans are often obsolete within hours or days of being written. The Strategy Note's one-page format comes with the recognition that recommendations will soon be out of date and should be acted upon quickly and re-assessed to ensure business momentum. Your written recommendations should be time-specific with a use-by date. Just before their use-by date, recommendations need to be reviewed.

LESSONS FROM CORONAVIRUS

British leader Boris Johnson initially recommended that people in Britain not socially distance and use a herd-immunity strategy with the Coronavirus. This recommendation carried unmitigated health risks, offered painful lessons and remained as the policy for less than a fortnight. Then, the advice changed and strict guidelines around social distancing were enforced. Boris Johnson was admitted to intensive care with the Coronavirus and was lucky to escape with his life. Fortunately for Johnson and Britain, he altered the recommendation in time. Coronavirus was a wake-up call for every leader on the planet. In a crisis, with billions in fear, this wake-up call revealed the real character of every leader.

China got the first wake-up call.

TASK ONE: WRITE YOUR RECOMMENDATION

The lockdown of one-billion people in China by Xi Jinping appeared to be a spectacular example of strategic alignment at work. Other countries' leaders did not respond as quickly, formulate a strategy as well, or align their citizens. Xi's rapid success in January 2020 was due to strategic clarity and execution.

Some businesses lack clarity when it comes to a coherent strategy and, others fall short of the necessary organizational compliance needed. Aligning people with strategy means having one or very few clear objectives and a trusted leader that provides timely recommendations. Successful leaders consult widely and often to stay ahead of the game. They formulate time-specific recommendations and review them regularly to ensure their organizations survive and thrive. There are dangers for governments, corporations, and businesses that operate without clear strategies and up to date recommendations.

TAKING CHARGE

Take a deep breath.

Now imagine an animal laboratory.

An almost motionless caged dog is receiving repeated electric shocks. This shaking creature has learned by trial and error that whichever moves she makes will result in the same shock! In the late 1960s, some unlucky dogs were subjects in a repeated series of electric shock experiments, where scientists showed that apathy and depression were the results of learned helplessness[8]. In a state of learned helplessness, the individual believes there is nothing they can do to remove themselves from a repeating adverse situation.

Early in the pandemic, intensive care doctors and nurses in high mortality hotspots, such as Long Island NY, reportedly experienced learned helplessness. With no end in sight, week after week, whatever they tried failed. Eventually, an overwhelmed Emergency Room (ER) doctor and a Emergency Room Technician (EMT) both suicided[9]. A tragic response to helplessness, not available to caged dogs. Many of us who did not suffer from COVID have nevertheless felt helpless and overwhelmed. We suffered varying levels of psychological fatigue from the daily stream of gloomy news reports from across the globe. In the end, every corner of the earth, including Antarctica, was placed on alert. Our brain's limbic system automatically keeps us on alert. In a protracted life and death situation, this reflexive part of our brain becomes highjacked.

Once highjacked, a feeling of being overwhelmed descends rapidly upon us and takes a firm hold. Panic buying of toilet paper, food and test kits point to such survival mechanisms. Our recommendations and actions become heavily influenced by our emergency 'fight or flight' modes, which are reflexive and reactive. Recommendations that are reflexive and reactive can be entirely appropriate at times. However, repeated reflexive thinking can be a trap. Unless we can shift mental gears at some point, reflexive thinking tends to increase fear and reduce creativity.

TASK ONE: WRITE YOUR RECOMMENDATION

Creativity and intuition are beneficial for a business. Intuition is accessible when we utilize reflective thinking. We can activate intuition by taking a warm shower or by embracing exercise, meditation, deep breathing, or listening to calming music.

INTUITION

What is your intuition about the future of your business?

What foresight do you have?

The way you see the future helps shape your approach.

Is your current approach strategic?

Your approach is strategic if it focusses on one or very few insightful objectives that lead to a cascade of benefits. Your approach should take the form of a recommendation, which is two or three sentences in length and reflects your insight and foresight.

What do I mean by insight and foresight?

Let me share two examples. In late 2019, just before publishing my first book, I wrote the following words.

'In tough economic times, with shallow water, like the early 2020s, careless big businesses easily ran aground.'

At that time, I knew that global debt was at record levels. Also, in my quieter moments, I felt that something big was just around the corner. Was that my intuition speaking gently? Jack Welch, legendary General Electric Chief Executive Officer (CEO) often spoke of trusting his 'gut' or intuition around future decision-making.

At that time, I also wrote, 'A great way to hedge your bets in the technology space, migrate value into your business and avoid the shocks associated with digital disruption, is to take an incremental approach with artificial intelligence and technology adoption."

The pandemic sank some businesses and favored others. The businesses which thrived had recently hedged their bets in the technology space, by taking a pro-active approach with artificial intelligence (AI) adoption. For example, bricks and mortar department stores failed and online retailers like Amazon flourished. With lockdown measures, companies that could be operated remotely and assisted by AI fared much better. I share these examples of insight and foresight, not to impress you but to impress upon you, that as leaders, in our quieter moments, we can have access to insight and foresight. Insight and foresight are important competencies we develop with accumulated experience, knowledge and our ability to stay present and become aware.

Our intuitive abilities still separate us from AI, for the time being. Taking time away from running your firm gives you time to gain insight and foresight. Paul, the overworked business owner, needed advice on how to allocate his time. He then cultivated the necessary insight and foresight to work on his business and improve his life.

TASK ONE: WRITE YOUR RECOMMENDATION

Different times and spaces are crucial ingredients for strategic planning. Successful leaders stay for days at a time, at a lakeside hideaway or mountain retreat with their entire board or executive team to nurture insight and cultivate foresight.

I will invite you to put this book down in a few moments.

If possible, take a relaxed walk in nature. Quieten your mind and tap into your intuitive wisdom. Take your leave with the intention of returning with an insightful recommendation for your business. One you might write down as the first task in creating your one-page strategy note.

Okay. Put this book down.

Enjoy.

ACTIVITY ONE
WRITE YOUR RECOMMENDATION

On your strategy note, the recommendation for your business should be written at the top of the page.

Write out in two or three sentences your current recommendation for your business for the coming month or quarter. An analysis or considerations of alternatives are not needed. At this point, write your current recommendation.

Lao Tzu once wrote, "The journey of a thousand miles begins with a single step."

Your recommendation provides a sense of what's next for the business from where you sit. I am going to encourage you to revisit your recommendation as we progress through each chapter. Each time you complete another task, you should revisit your recommendation.

Some examples of recommendations might be:

'Find a regional or local supplier to reduce our over-reliance on China. Give the local supplier 40% of the sourcing of our materials.'

'Explore options available for covering the payment of our recently failed lawsuit. Include discussions with our accountants, lawyers,

TASK ONE: WRITE YOUR RECOMMENDATION

bankers and the securities commission for both debt and equity raising options.'

'Extend the reach of our global market. Invite tenders from eighty potential distributors and resellers in Beijing, Berlin, Dallas, Dubai, London, Santiago, Singapore and St Petersburg.'

'Recruit secretarial support for the Board and the CFO at this time. Move a 'lack of confidence' vote in Terry Troublemaker and invite his fellow board members to request his resignation. If successful, appoint a new board member using our new diversity policy.'

'Split our agency of 350 employees into four autonomous regional service groups. Remove one layer of management. Reduce red tape, increase efficiency and enhance public value.'

'Ask the CEO if she would like to renew her contract in twelve months-time, under the same terms. If not, ask the Human Resources Manager to start making up a list of possible candidates, so that we have a Plan B.'

It's time to write. Jot down your current recommendation for your business.

THE STRATEGY NOTE

STRATEGY NOTE - JUNE QUARTER

1. RECOMMENDATION

"Brevity is the best recommendation."

Cicero

TASK TWO
REPORT YOUR HEALTH

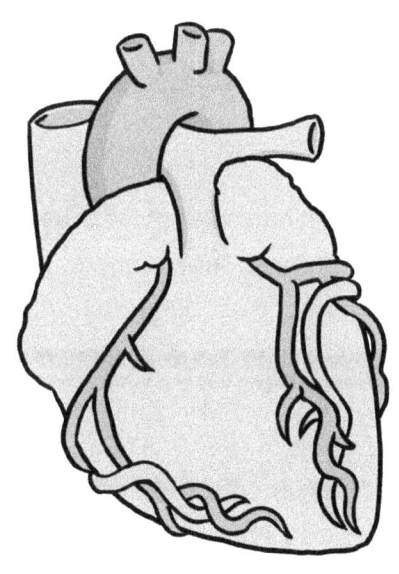

THE STRATEGY NOTE

TASK TWO
REPORT YOUR HEALTH

I dampened the throttle on my BMW sports bike. The road ahead looked bumpy and uneven. Chuck's Harley Davidson cruiser thundered past, right over the potholes.

I wondered if his approach to the road carried over into business.

Fifty years ago, Chuck's father Jim established Prestige Motorcycles. Ten years ago, Jim left operating the business to Chuck. Prestige had forty employees working in five departments across two sites: new bike sales; helmets and accessories; used bike sales; service and the body shop.

Chuck invited me to help him sort out what he described as 'people problems'. Once I interviewed his people, I discovered some of Chuck's managers did not trust him. When I probed further, they shared that Chuck was not honest with them about what happened in the business.

They revealed that worker safety in some departments was well below par. There was also a policy that required accidental damage to motor bikes being worked on or handled by staff to be taken out of their wages. Repair costs were deducted at market rates, despite the business having a body shop that could do the repairs at cost.

TASK TWO: REPORT YOUR HEALTH

I wondered why an outwardly successful business, which enjoyed a monopoly market position, would need to penny-pinch on working conditions, safety and salaries.

I asked Chuck to show me the financial statements for the last three years. Chuck said he did not know much about them and suggested I ask Jody from the accounts department for them.

Who is running your business right now?

How healthy are they?

Imagine your business is a ship with a captain and crew. It might be a sailing boat, container, tanker, naval frigate, galleon, ferry, cruise ship, special purpose vessel or perhaps a submarine. Above and below deck could be uniformed account managers and a motley crew of software developers.

Is your crew fit for purpose?

Do they perform well in a storm?

Are there icebergs?

Could you be the owner of the Titanic on a dark night?

I want to introduce the metaphors of fitness and health to help you assess and report on the condition of your ship, its officers and crew.

When I board a client's ship, I ask to meet their financial officer and see three years-worth of financial statements, to get a sense of their ship's strength. I also make a note of the current economic tides. An emptying tide strands all boats. A rising tide is best at lifting the biggest ships, especially if they have adequate reserves and no debt.

FINANCIAL RATIOS

Amid rough seas and strong winds, firms with low debt to equity ratios are likely to remain afloat. They have the reserves needed to navigate successfully and build new capabilities. The amount of money borrowed divided by the firm's market value is the Debt to Equity [DE] ratio. With many companies, this ratio is not made public. Astute investors must sift through annual reports to uncover the level of company debt.

The safest debt level is zero. A firm with no debt is like a person with a healthy beating heart. Hearty companies like Apple are debt-free with high market values. Hence Apple has a DE ratio of zero. As the DE ratio climbs above 30%, or 0.3, levels of risk must be understood and articulated. It is not unusual for promising start-ups to have DE ratios of 4 or greater. Large banks and financial institutions that are backed by governments, often operate with DE ratios between 2 and 5.

For a mature business, a high ratio reveals a compromised heart and potential co-morbidities. During a financial crisis, 'heart attacks' are frequent, and bank DE ratios can reach 10 or greater. Once this occurs, such banks are 'too big to fail' and often receive emergency transfusions from governments. Strategic choices need to be understood and implemented with an awareness of the overall health of the business. It is for this reason that the DE ratio is the first financial health measure to be recorded in a strategy note. Board members, CEOs, business owners and leaders must regularly obtain DE ratios from their CFO or accountant.

Your CFO or accountant should also be able to provide you with a Quick Ratio [QR]. The QR is the second financial health measure that must be recorded in the strategy note. Your QR measures the financial fitness of your firm. Your QR measures your firm's ability to meet its short-term obligations using its most liquid assets. The QR is an acid test that determines short-term liquidity and provides a measure of your firm's financial fitness or weakness. A fit firm can meet its current obligations quickly. A weak firm will drag its feet.

QR = (Current Assets – Inventories) / (Current Liabilities).

Firms that operate with no inventory or with just-in-time inventory are fitter than firms that carry extensive stockpiles. Large stockpiles can take months or years to turnover and are usually hard to liquidate quickly. High flying manufacturers like Boeing hold inventory items for months or years. By contrast, down to earth wholesalers like Costco, turn their inventory more rapidly. Boeing's QR at the start of 2020 was 0.25. Costco's was twice that at 0.5. The higher the QR, the fitter the firm. Because Uber has no fleet and little inventory, its QR is 2.0. A commonly acceptable QR is 1.0. If the QR is less than 1.0, a company may be unable to pay its bills. However, acceptable ranges vary from industry to industry. For example, organic food growers have little inventory and few bills to pay. Consequently, they enjoy high levels of fitness and good short-term liquidity, with QRs of 4.0 or greater.

Healthy looking firms with little or no inventory may have hidden current liabilities, such as growing capital gains tax liabilities, accumulated employee long-service leave, annual leave, and sick leave entitlements, which lowers their QR. When Bill Gates was at Microsoft, he solved this issue by ensuring that the company always had a full year's payroll in reserve. When a firm's current assets include generous reserves of cash and marketable securities, this raises the QR. If these firms import goods, they will do well to make foreign currency exchanges when their local dollar is strong relative to the world. Firms with ample cash reserves often set up a series of staggered multi-year rolling term deposits to balance returns on cash with ongoing liquidity demands.

Once I spend time aboard a client's ship and gauge their fitness, we discover whether there are sufficient resources above and below deck. Financial fitness supports a healthy continuation of the existing strategy or a change in policy.

We then assess the leadership. We examine the wisdom of the captain and officers. Are they seasoned and seaworthy? What have they learned along the way?

Next up, we assess the client's strategic competence, organizational structure, systems, and the crew. I often complete a cultural audit via employee interviews. Some crew members are mutineers. Others fight. A few are there for a free ride. Some jump ship at the first sign of trouble. The best crews trust the leadership of their captain, the ship's officers and other crew members.

LEADERSHIP SCORE

A business risks becoming impotent without people who believe in its leader. Leaders with a tribe who believe in them, have an advantage over other leaders. Before people can believe in a leader, there needs to be a foundation of trust. People trust leaders with whom they have a good connection and who create conditions for employees to realize their potential. At a practical level, employees look for a leader who can communicate and deliver strategy effectively.

In your firm, how often do employees trust the leader?

Is it essential that they do?

Give the leader a score out of 10.

To help score the leader, you might use a 360-degree assessment that records vital stakeholder views around leadership **authenticity**, **competence** and **empathy**. A lack of trust in the leader can hurt the strategy. Adding a leadership trust score to the strategy note can help the leader and improve the business. If we continue with the health metaphor, confidence in one's leader is akin to having good mental health within the business. If you are having trouble coming up with a valid and reliable leadership score, you owe it to your firm and your future success to calculate one. Some unbiased research about the leader is needed.

Incompetent, inauthentic and indifferent leaders are everywhere, especially in politics. Competent but inauthentic leaders tend to have a finite life. Competent, authentic, but harsh leaders are often very successful, especially in the early stages of business growth. Yet such aggressive leaders can be downright mean.

Who was the best leader Apple ever had?

Tim Cook or Steve Jobs?

Scratch below the surface, and you'll find that as well as being aggressive and obsessed with design quality, elegance, and functionality, at times, Steve Jobs was harsh and lacked empathy[10]. This lack of empathy and harshness is common in leaders of early-stage tech companies. Andy Grove from Intel and Elon Musk from Tesla have reputations for being obsessive and harsh leaders. Add to the mix, Uber founder Travis Kalanick, who admits he 'enjoys pissing people off.' Yet, Travis's aggression allowed Uber to break formidable regulatory barriers to entry. In his early years, Bill Gates was obsessive and sometimes drove his project leaders to chronic fatigue and even insanity.

By contrast, as a humble leader, Tim Cook seems competent, authentic, and empathic. Recent studies reveal humble leaders foster more-collaborative top management teams, model participatory leadership, increase information sharing across the organization, and realize superior market returns[11]. Good companies become great when their leaders embody humility[12]. Recently appointed Uber CEO, Dara Khosrowshahi embodies competency, empathy and an elevated level of authenticity. The right tonic for transforming Uber's problematic *frat boy* culture and putting it on a path from good to great[13].

The timing of Tim Cook's appointment aligned well when Apple needed to grow from good to great. Trust in your leaders will change over time. As a business evolves, trust in early leaders may decrease, and trust in more humble leaders may increase. Having a leader whose leadership style matches your stage of business growth can have a significant impact on how much a tribe trusts the leader and how well the business performs.

TRIBE SCORE

In a tribe or workforce, group identity and social recognition give rise to high levels of affiliation, co-operation and positive mental health. There are parallels here between a healthy workforce and a healthy body. Today, organizations understand more about the balance of ingredients that make up a healthy workforce. For example, for many men, women, and LGBTQIA people, safety, security, diversity, and self-esteem have become foundational considerations.

A balanced, yet personalized diet, with a variety of plant-based foods, is necessary for a healthy body. Balanced teams, personalized for a business, with a variety of talented people, are necessary for a healthy workforce. However, once out of balance, both systems deteriorate. A symbiotic relationship exists between one's mind and body – and between a leader and their tribe. They feed off each other. Knowing the leader's trust in their tribe and the tribe's trust in their leader are essential.

As a leader, do you believe that your people can deliver on the strategy?

How important is it that people deliver?

Give your people a score out of 10.

A leader's trust in their tribe can help their tribe's performance. For this reason, reporting a high tribe score in your strategy note can be helpful. If your tribe score is low, highlighting it in the strategy note can hurt or help your tribe's performance. Care is needed. For most teams, letting the tribe know that you believe in them is the best policy. Teams receiving low tribe scores can react differently. For some teams, failure is not the best teacher. Here the team will internalize a low score in a way that reduces their overall confidence and ability. To improve performance in such teams, highlighting existing strengths to be improved, can have a positive effect. Empathic leaders often take this approach to improve results[14].

More experienced teams, with a growth mindset[15], will understand that their abilities are not fixed and can be improved. For these teams, a low tribe score offers them an incentive to grow and failure can be an effective teacher. At times, not everyone at Apple liked Steve Jobs. However, deep down, Steve believed in his people. Steve had faith in his diverse and talented tribe. Employees knew that when Steve lost confidence in one of his leaders, they were dismissed. So, if you were still employed, Steve had faith in you[16]. Having a top leadership score and a high tribe score helps to create a prosperous business.

Three weeks after asking Jody for Prestige's financial statements, I called Chuck. Chuck had just returned from another extravagant 'business trip' to Macau. I dropped by Chuck's office to collect the statements. Before handing them to me, Chuck said that last month, he had secured a five-hundred-thousand-dollar mortgage against his home. A transaction that would not appear in the financial statements. He claimed that he needed the extra funds to clear some bad debts and stock the business with the coming year's bike models.

A quick examination of Prestige's balance sheet revealed total assets of 12 million and total liabilities of 24 million. Prestige had a DE ratio of 2.0. This ratio explained why Chuck had mortgaged his home. No sane bank would lend the business money at this point.

I looked down the list of assets. Assets included land, buildings, plant and equipment valued at $8 million. Further down was inventory worth $3.5 million. An inventory figure equal to approximately 250 bikes. I was confused. Showroom stock at any one time was 40 bikes and the used bike outlet had 20 bikes. The helmets, accessories and body shop inventories between them couldn't be worth more than $0.3 million.

Prestige's current liabilities, including overdue payments to numerous suppliers, totaled $1 million. Their current assets, including monies currently owed to the business by dozens of delinquent celebrity customers, topped $0.6 million.

Prestige's QR was ($0.6 million - $3.5 million) / ($1 million) = minus 2.9!

QRs in the cut-throat motor industry sometimes fall below zero, but not that far.

I enquired, "Chuck, where is the $3.5 million of inventory?"

Chuck explained that his father liked having only current model bikes on the showroom floor. So, over the last ten years, Chuck stored all the previous years' unsold bikes in a giant shed behind the body shop. Each year, Chuck instructed the accountant not to depreciate the growing and aging stock of bikes and leave their values unchanged. Chuck hoped that in time the bikes might become collectors' items. Meanwhile, his gamble meant liquidity in the business suffered and the level of debt kept increasing.

As I worked more closely with Chuck, I discovered that his trips to Asia were less about meeting suppliers and more about wild nights in Macau. Sadly, Chuck had a gambling and drug addiction, and he was neither healthy nor fit enough to lead the business.

TASK TWO: REPORT YOUR HEALTH

The second lesson I took from TJ is that during prosperous times, danger lurks for every business. Growth masks waste, extravagance, and inefficiency. The Strategy Note's requirement to continuously and transparently report debt, liquidity, leadership and tribe scores will help a business avoid unhealthy surprises.

THE STRATEGY NOTE

ACTIVITY TWO
REPORT YOUR HEALTH

It's time to revisit your recommendation in light of your ratios and scores. On your strategy note, in the space below your recommendation, write out your two ratios and your two scores.

DE Ratio: QR: Leadership Score: Tribe Score:

Reflect on your ratios and scores. Each of these ratios and scores move over time. Changes to your balance sheet, your profit and loss statement, trust in your leadership, and faith in your people all have an impact on your company's health.

How do you feel about your four health numbers?

Do you get a sense that your business's health is better than ever, or has it deteriorated in recent months or years? Which health numbers are encouraging? Are you happy to be sharing all these scores with others via the strategy note?

Which health numbers could be improved?

Is your recommendation still appropriate? Should you modify it in light of the ratios and scores you have just reported?

TASK TWO: REPORT YOUR HEALTH

If this health assessment has uncovered a vital people or financial issue, it is important to defer your initial recommendation and write a recommendation that addresses the issue.

Should your recommendation address debt, profitability, leadership, or employee performance in a more targeted way?

There is little point setting sail for a new destination, if the ship or crew are not healthy.

Your one-page strategy note should help you move faster with influence. Reporting your health to stakeholders, via your strategy note in a transparent way, may prove painful at first. Not reporting your health can make you feel safer in the short-term. But this is false security. In the long term, lack of reporting spells disaster. The sins of the past are revealed all the way to the bottom line.

If necessary, update your recommendation now.

THE STRATEGY NOTE

STRATEGY NOTE – JUNE QUARTER

1. RECOMMENDATION

2. DEBT SCORE   QUICK SCORE   LEADER SCORE   TRIBE SCORE

"Beware of little expenses. A small leak will sink a great ship."

Benjamin Franklin

TASK THREE

SUMMARIZE YOUR ANALYSIS

THE STRATEGY NOTE

TASK THREE
SUMMARIZE YOUR ANALYSIS

Analyzing the behavior of people who purchase books reveals that half of those who start reading a book, never get past the third chapter. As reading progresses, readers thin out. Less than a third of people finish the books they start.

If you are still reading this book, what advice are you seeking?

If your interest is waning, perhaps write recommendations that help your business grow using the 4Bs. In other words, try to build a bigger, better, brighter or bolder business. To grow, it helps to have an understanding of your industry, its critical success factors, your claim to fame, and a clear picture of your relationship with customers. To succeed at the 4B game, you must sharpen your pencil and discover bright new ways to serve more customers, develop better products and services and take bold steps with technology to build a bigger business.

WIDE ANGLE LENS

As your industry matures and customers settle or leave, the number of players narrows. Businesses that capture the most customers enjoy increasing returns from scale. Industry consolidation results

TASK THREE: SUMMARIZE YOUR ANALYSIS

in winners and losers. Is your business winning or losing right now? What is the best way to get a picture of what's happening? The camera that best captures a strategic snapshot is the camera with a wide-angle lens. A wide-angle shot helps us see the immediate future as well as what is happening around us. Futurists take to the world with a telephoto lens. A telephoto lens gives them a long-range shot of a narrow piece of information on the distant horizon. The long-range telephoto shot offers clues to system-wide changes, that are still years away.

Unlike wide-angle shots, telephoto shots offer very little immediate contextual value. Your accountant probably looks at your business with a microscope in hand. A microscopic view of your business can give you a helpful understanding of the past. Yet this view offers limited wisdom about current events. To take a wide-angle snapshot, focus on the real world of customers, markets and emerging digital competition. As you do, you may start to ask some compelling questions.

'Why does our firm still exist?'

'Are we still needed?'

In the beginning, after some initial analysis, someone, perhaps you, decided to create the business, firm or organization. Analysis that supports your decision to continue with the business, or sell it also needs to be done from time to time. Before industries start contracting, firms must reinvent themselves using the 4Bs.

Reinvention has always been at the heart of 3M. 3M is a significant global corporation operating in the health care, worker safety and consumer goods markets. 3M started life as Minnesota Mining and Manufacturing, a small quarry mining business. Coca-Cola started as a boutique pharmaceutical company. Apple made circuit boards for geeks and home-computer builders. Historically, each of these firms enhanced their picture of the world at regular intervals. Each was prepared to reimagine a bigger, better, brighter and bolder future, based on their ongoing analysis and the new pictures that emerged.

SELL THE MILLS

Timely analysis allows a firm to pivot before it reaches the end of its economic life. Sometimes pivoting means transferring a well-developed capability from one setting to another. Other times, pivoting means letting go of the traditional business model and boldly embracing a new one. Darwin Smith, the courageous Kimberly Clark CEO, was ridiculed by the media when he led the sale of the company's paper mills and shifted its focus to the end-consumer. Kimberly Clark created the Kleenex and Huggies brands that ultimately outperformed Procter & Gamble in the market[17].

Phrases like 'burn the boats,' 'sink the ships' and 'sell the mills' are used to describe leaders that radically transform a business. Darwin Smith analyzed the industry supply chain and worked out there was far greater profitability in moving away from paper milling and towards consumer products. Apple analyzed its home-computer

TASK THREE: SUMMARIZE YOUR ANALYSIS

builder market and compared that with its analysis of the potential user market in schools, universities and businesses. The founders of Coca-Cola were morphine and opium addicts. They initially manufactured Coke that contained 9mg of cocaine per glass[18]. When government analysis of Coke's ingredients was carried out, cocaine levels were rapidly minimized and subsequently eliminated. They were forced to pivot.

What big changes have forced your business to pivot in some way?

Did your customers' needs change?

Does your business need to be bigger, better, brighter or bolder?

Which emphasis will be more important in future? Which of the 4Bs will be least relevant? Why?

YOUR ANALYSIS

What analysis is needed to validate your current business approach or to challenge it?

As the strategy note is written on a single page, there is not enough room to record a full analysis. Instead, this part of the strategy note requires you to write a summary of your analysis. Your summary could draw upon any number of sources. This might include the projected impact of a new industry or government regulation. It might consist of findings from an intelligence report that reveals industry-wide changes in sales, profitability, and market shares. It might include conclusions from an internal team or consultancy. There may be findings regarding your supply chain and the new role artificial intelligence and automation are set to play in your industry. It might include test results from an analytical tool used in your business. It might consist of insights from a competitor's annual report, your Customer Relationship Management System activity or analysis of your production schedule.

If you own a copy of The Strategy Book[19], it may be useful to revisit some of the analytical tools it contains. The Strategy Book helps you create a strategic mindset and complete a structured analysis. It includes analytical frameworks like Industry Attractiveness, Claim to Fame, Critical Success Factors and the Customer Intimacy Wheel. When completing your analysis, choosing the right analytical frameworks is critical. Each framework poses a set of questions. The most successful businesses concern themselves with finding the right questions to ask. They are less concerned with getting the right answers to the wrong questions.

Joseph Campbell, the great chronicler of The Hero's Journey[20], reminds us that asking the right questions will ensure our ladder is resting against the right wall. If our ladder is not leaning on the right wall, in time, we will get further and further away from where we should be. I encourage you to use your most challenging and proven processes for this analysis task. If the analysis process is new to you, I'd suggest you start with these four straight-forward analytical frameworks which are included in the appendix section of this book.

TASK THREE: SUMMARIZE YOUR ANALYSIS

Appendix A. Industry Attractiveness
Appendix B. Claim to Fame
Appendix C. Critical Success Factors
Appendix D. Customer Intimacy Wheel

Industry Attractiveness

In a sentence or two, it can be helpful to summarize the attractiveness of your industry and any changes you expect in the future. Adding your Industry Attractiveness to the summary in your strategy note gives you and your reader a useful context for your recommendation.

Claim to Fame

If you know the Claim to Fame of your firm, write it in a sentence. Adding your Claim to Fame to your strategy note will remind you and your reader of your business's unique capabilities, value proposition and reputation. Revisit your firm's current strategy. Does it uphold and maximize your Claim to Fame?

Critical Success Factors

Including the Critical Success Factors for all players in your industry in your strategy note is a good idea. Adding your performance scores on these success factors will remind you of the things you must focus on to remain successful. Your recommendation should be written with an awareness of your industry's Critical Success Factors, and it may even address one of these factors specifically. Just to re-iterate, your strategy note's recommendation reveals the most important thing or combination of things you should be focussed on in the short-term to remain successful in the long-run.

Customer Intimacy Wheel

The Customer Intimacy Wheel reveals the depth of your relationship with customers. Do your customers see you as merely a product provider? If so, how might you better sell the benefits, build better two-way relationships with your customers or even convert them to value-adding alliance partners?

As you undertake your analysis, keep the 4Bs in mind. What questions can you ask that will help you grow a bigger, better, brighter and bolder business? Proper analysis leads to valuable insights. As the patterns and answers emerge, summarize the most helpful findings in your strategy note. Your summary should reveal bright new ways to serve more customers, develop better products and services, and take bold steps with technology to scale your business.

TASK THREE: SUMMARIZE YOUR ANALYSIS

ACTIVITY THREE
SUMMARIZE YOUR ANALYSIS

Summarize your analysis a fifth of the way down the one-page strategy note. If your analysis included an Industry Attractiveness assessment, confirmation of your Claim to Fame or scoring your performance on Critical Success Factors or an examination of the Customer Intimacy Wheel, include these in your summary.

To support your summary, you may like to create a series of appendices that contain things like projected cash flows, employee survey results, industry reports, executive reviews and financial ratios from your industry. Appendices must support your summary. Ideally, your strategy note should not have appendices. It should deliver your recommendation, health scores and an overview of your analysis. If you include appendices, do so sparingly. Your strategy note should help people move faster with influence, not engage in paralysis by analysis.

It's time to write.

Write two or three short paragraphs, that occupy no more than one-quarter of a page in length.

How does your summary make you feel about your firm's future? Do you get a sense that the business environment is fiercer than ever, or has the business environment improved recently? Is your brand reputation still good? What threats, opportunities and industry changes are ahead?

Which critical success factors could you perform better? How do players in your industry perform on these critical success factors?

Are your customers simply product purchasers? Or are they highly satisfied clients, loyal members of your brand's growing community, or value-adding alliance partners?

Is your recommendation at the top of the page still appropriate? In light of your analysis, should you modify your recommendation?

If necessary, update your recommendation now.

TASK THREE: SUMMARIZE YOUR ANALYSIS

STRATEGY NOTE - JUNE QUARTER

1. RECOMMENDATION

2. DEBT SCORE   QUICK SCORE   LEADER SCORE   TRIBE SCORE

3. ANALYSIS

"Get closer than ever to your customers. So close that you tell them what they need well before they realize it themselves."

Steve Jobs

TASK FOUR

NAME YOUR OPTIONS

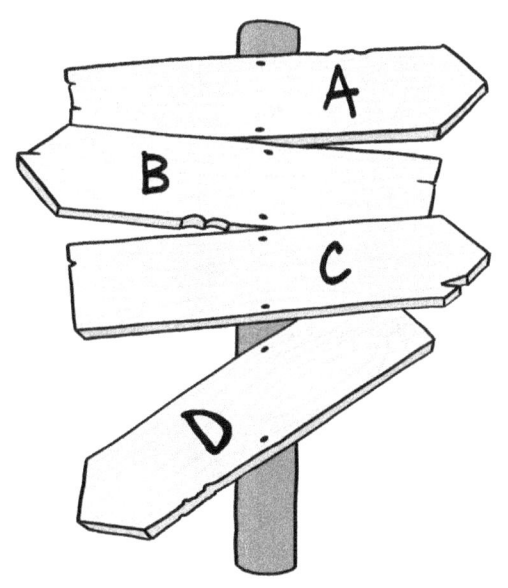

TASK FOUR
NAME YOUR OPTIONS

When I was growing up, I heard my father say, "A choice of one is no choice at all."

My mother would say, "Walk a mile in other people's shoes. It helps you to make a difference."

People and events in your life have helped shape the way you see the world. As life changes, you can change the way you approach life. As a teenager, I experienced the rewards of keeping my options alive and placing myself in another's shoes.

LIFESAVING

One summer afternoon, when I was fourteen, my friends and I were in a group swimming near the river mouth, when the current caught us. We swam and swam and managed to get to shore and, as we crawled up the sand exhausted, and barely able to breathe, we saw that our mate Bernard was still out there. He was a long way from shore and being carried further out. He was stuck, exhausted, struggling and probably not going to make it unless someone saved him. But who? We were exhausted, and

TASK FOUR: NAME YOUR OPTIONS

the current was strong. Our first option was to alert the rescue services back in town. However, they were out of range.

Bernard was now a long way out and starting to panic. What if we ran along the riverbank and found a boat up-stream? We sent Brett, still out of breath, to look for a boat. Like the others, I was exhausted, but starting to recover. Bernard was out of gas, and he started disappearing below the water. I saw that the situation was life-threatening. How could we rescue Bernard? What if I mustered my remaining energy, swam into the current, grabbed Bernard and then guided him back to safety?

Another option was to avoid two drownings by staying put.

I chose the first option and plunged in. I swam with all my remaining might and got to Bernard, who was floundering and panicking. I kept my distance at first. I knew that desperate drowning people can lock onto their rescuer in a way that will drown them both. Treading water from a distance, I assessed Bernard. He looked pleased to see me, but there was a weird and visceral look of desperation in his eyes. I still had the option not to rescue Bernard. I assured Bernard that I would help him if he listened carefully. Bernard's leg was cramping, and he was too exhausted to swim. I got Bernard in a hold, and with him kicking with his good leg, together we swam across the current. We gradually struggled back to shore, broken but alive.

Looking back, I can see that I was forced to keep adapting my strategy for the changing circumstances.

In business, continually creating options and even combining them ensures that we survive and thrive. Thriving businesses have leaders who routinely ask, "what if" questions and give themselves options. In 1996, Steve Jobs returned to a drowning Apple. A year later, Apple was saved from bankruptcy after Bill Gates injected $150M of equity and free access to Microsoft Office. Steve then gave himself two options. One option was to build the biggest computer in the world and rent space on it. The other option was to build small personal devices and sell them to everybody. In many ways, building a single supercomputer was more straight-forward than building and shipping 200 million iPhones per annum.

However, Steve decided that placing a device in our hands was less risky and more rewarding than placing a supercomputer somewhere in the desert and trying to connect us to it. Eventually, he did both by creating iCloud.

Choosing smart options can make a world of difference to your business and the wider world. Having generous friends like Bill can also help. Upon retiring from Microsoft, Bill Gates and his wife established The Bill and Melinda Gates Foundation, which has polio virus eradication as one of its top priorities.

In 2015, citing lessons learned from West Africa's Ebola crisis, Bill said that the United States and other countries were not prepared for the future virus that was going to hit them.

Bill shared, "If anything kills over 10 million people in the next few decades, it's most likely to be a highly infectious virus rather than a war, not missiles, but microbes. We've actually invested very little in a system to stop an epidemic."[21]

Bill added, "We're not ready for the next epidemic!"

Our unprepared world had not considered Coronavirus a real threat, until it nestled into in our cruise ships, hospitals and morgues.

Bill was right.

FUTURE OPTIONS

What are the future strategic options for your business?

Your strategy note must fit on a single page. So, there is not enough room to unpack all possible options. Instead, the strategy note requires you to choose your best approach. This approach is your Plan A, and it should align with your written recommendation. It is helpful to record Plan B, Plan C and Plan D options by name, with a brief description. For many businesses, Plan A is their conventional or official approach. For those businesses, there are no other alternatives.

If there is an understanding of alternative plans within your business, then naming each in your strategy note will be straightforward. For example, imagine you are a crop farmer. Your Plan A or default approach is to spell, plough, sow, grow and harvest for a profit. Plan B could be to lease even more land in response to expected wet seasons, sow more grains and then harvest a bumper mature crop. Plan C could be to harvest immature crops early during an extended dry spell. Plan D could be the option to not plant in the midst of a multi-year drought.

Do you have well-understood options for your business?

How will you decide between them?

DECISION TOOLS

While there are many ways you could come up with options, some helpful ways involve Scenario Planning, Decision Trees and the calculation of Expected Monetary Values. These three decision tools, along with a business example, are included in the appendix section of this book.

Appendix E.   Scenario Planning
Appendix F.   Decision Trees
Appendix G.   Expected Monetary Values

Scenario Planning

The future belongs to those businesses that see possibilities before they become apparent. Doing this usually involves Scenario Planning. Appropriately done, Scenario Planning requires you to create five

TASK FOUR: NAME YOUR OPTIONS

imaginative stories about the future. This is what Bill Gates tried to do with the idea of a future pandemic.

1. The Official Future Scenario
2. A More of the Same but Much Worse Scenario
3. A More of the Same but Much Better Scenario
4. A Different and Much Worse Scenario
5. A Different and Much Better Scenario

You will find examples of the five scenarios in Appendix E.

Seeing change earlier means you can start responding sooner or capitalise faster on new opportunities. A good example might be China at the start of 2020. China had previously experienced virus outbreaks, like SARS and MERS. As soon as they saw the rapid spread of the Coronavirus, they moved at lightning speed to build new mega hospitals and sent an envoy abroad to purchase extra face masks[22]. The US Federal Reserve Bank remembered recent stock market collapses, like the Global Financial Crisis (GFC). This time the Fed acted in days, not months, with quantitative easing to sure-up at-risk banks and investment houses.

Now I'm going to contradict myself.

At least half of the time, Scenario Planning does not work!

Why?

Because the truth is, as Bill Gates discovered, we are terrible at listening to scenarios about a disaster. It is more likely that both China and the US Federal Reserve had not done much in the way of Scenario Planning. China and the Fed reacted quickly not because of their Scenario Planning efforts, but because of their lack of preparedness in recent years with SARS and the GFC. A lack of Scenario Planning is the reason why rolling food shortages in China played out in 2020. The pandemic death toll and sweeping social unrest in the United States, revealed that both governors and the White House had been terrible at listening to scenarios about disaster.

Because we are terrible at listening to scenarios about disasters, we often avoid naming and telling ourselves the Different but Much Worse and the Same but Much Worse Scenarios. Disastrous scenarios often have low probabilities. Nevertheless, naming these worse case scenarios and understanding their symptoms can help us mitigate risk quickly and capitalize on opportunity, in the event of a catastrophic disaster.

Decision Trees and Expected Monetary Values

If you have a number of options for your business and you are not yet sure which option to take, Decision Trees and Expected Monetary Values can help. There are worked examples of each in appendices F and G. Once you understand how to draw a Decision Tree and calculate the Expected Monetary Values of various options, choosing the best option should prove easier.

TASK FOUR: NAME YOUR OPTIONS

ACTIVITY FOUR
NAME YOUR OPTIONS

Half-way down the page of your one-page strategy note, name your options and highlight your best option.

You will need to articulate your best option, Plan A, in two to three sentences. Then, I recommend that you dedicate a sentence or two for Plan B, Plan C and Plan D. Naming your four options should occupy no more than one-fifth of a page.

It can help to create a series of appendices that contain your scenarios, decision trees and expected monetary value calculations. The appendices can then be attached to your strategy note. Ideally, a one-page strategy note should not have appendices. It should deliver your recommendation, health scores, analysis summary, and options. Your readers need to understand and act quickly. If you decide to include appendices, do so sparingly. The goal of the one-page strategy note is to help your business move faster with influence.

It's time to write. Name your options.

Name your Plan A. Then provide a summary of your Plan A and name the alternatives you considered. Naming your Plan B, C and D alternatives will serve as a blind-spot check so that you have more, not less confidence, in your preferred approach.

Is your recommendation at the top of your strategy note still appropriate?

Should you modify it in light of the scenarios, decision trees and expected monetary values you may have developed? How might your recommendation better reflect your preferred option?

If needed, update your recommendation now.

TASK FOUR: NAME YOUR OPTIONS

```
STRATEGY NOTE - JUNE QUARTER

1. RECOMMENDATION


2. DEBT SCORE   QUICK SCORE   LEADER SCORE   TRIBE SCORE

3. ANALYSIS




4. OPTIONS
```

"I always say don't make plans, make options."

Jennifer Aniston

STEP FIVE

GROW DIGITAL WINGS

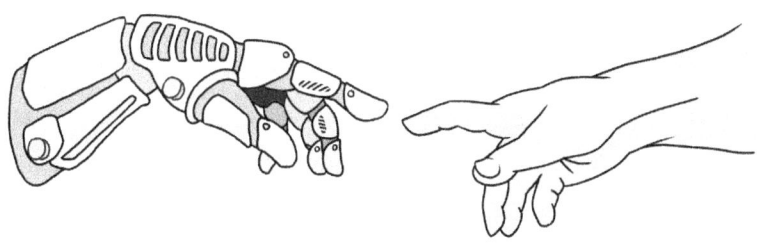

THE STRATEGY NOTE

TASK FIVE
GROW DIGITAL WINGS

With advancing digital change, your business may experience a quick death or a slow demise.

Or will your business reinvent itself?

LIFE AND DEATH

Five hundred years ago, during China's Ming Dynasty, public execution regressed from death by one-hundred cuts to death by one-thousand cuts[23]. A prolonged, excruciating demise. Recently, we have seen death by one thousand cuts for hundreds of bricks-and-mortar businesses, like Blockbuster, Borders and Sears[24]. This is being driven by automation, cost competition and the digital capture of customers by firms that have grown digital wings.

During the Italian Renaissance in 1510, Michelangelo painted the life-giving 'Creation of Adam' in the Sistine Chapel. I want you to use the strategy note to give new life to your business. Five hundred years on from the Ming Dynasty and the Italian Renaissance, we are in a new Renaissance period. In 2010, AI was given new life as it became smarter, cheaper and much less avoidable. In 2010, Google introduced personalized search results and a year later, Apple gave birth to Siri. From Uber ride sharing to robotic fruit pickers and machine-learning-hedge-fund-managers, the Digital Renaissance has arrived.

DIGITAL WINGS

New machines are not just coming up with answers. They are finding the questions. Supercomputers, big data and machine learning are predicting many of life's events before they happen. Today, your business needs a vision for success in the digital economy. AI means that roles in professional services for accountants, lawyers, doctors, cartographers, analysts and salespeople are dwindling. On the other hand, roles for human resource managers, chief executives, event planners, writers, graphic designers and software developers are safe for now. As the line between human and artificial intelligence merges, I see that people are beginning to think more like computers, becoming lazy, or both. AI is allowing powerful nations, like China, greater societal monitoring and the advancement of anti-democratic agendas[25].

So, what does this merging with technology mean for you?

If your firm has the wrong strategy, technology can be a doubled edged sword. New technology may help your firm correct strategy sooner. It can also hasten the demise of a firm with the wrong strategy.

Throughout history, advancing technology has intersected with changes in society[26]. Staying aware of technology and listening to the whispers of changing societal needs can reveal what's next for your business. With the Digital Renaissance, we will continue to see new entrants with new business models and existing businesses crossing into new industries. To survive, firms must take a market approach, rather than a specific industry focus. New entrants include neo-banks, mobile wallets and evolved 'love at first swipe' dating apps. Amazon began in the book industry. Amazon then crossed over into other industries by taking a market approach.

Uber entered the hallowed taxi industry with rideshare. Instead of staying in the taxi space, they kept taking a market approach. They moved into meal delivery, freight, high-end limousines, bike and scooter hire. Uber also places shift workers in food production, warehouse, events, and customer service. Uber has literally grown digital wings with vertical take-off-and-landing aircraft in Melbourne, Dallas and Los Angeles. With such societal upheaval, making a case for your digitally-driven future enterprise can be hard, and giving up can seem easier. Nevertheless, a recent study by MIT's Sloan Centre for Information Systems Research, revealed that just 24% of boards of large public companies were digitally savy. The research showed that the companies of digitally savy boards, outperformed the remaining 76% of firms by 34%, in both revenue and return on investment[27].

I encourage you not to give up. Instead, double down on your research and development. Research the market, not just your industry. Develop an intimate understanding of your customers' existing and anticipated needs. Figure out better ways to serve and service them. Look for the ways new technology might intersect with societal needs. Seriously consider fringe innovations, including ones that seem technically unfeasible today. Winning with technology is largely about change. Your ability to quickly adapt to it is crucial. In the coming decade, you can influence your business by using strategy notes to switch markets, grow digital wings, and reinvent your business.

The functional value of technology increases as your business grows. You can think about the business value of technology in terms of five digital wings.

1. Reach – connections across geographic and virtual domains
2. Richness – the usefulness of data and information
3. Response – speed in which information is delivered to the user
4. Range – the breadth of functionality within an integrated system
5. Removal – automation that eliminates people, pain and processes

THE STRATEGY NOTE

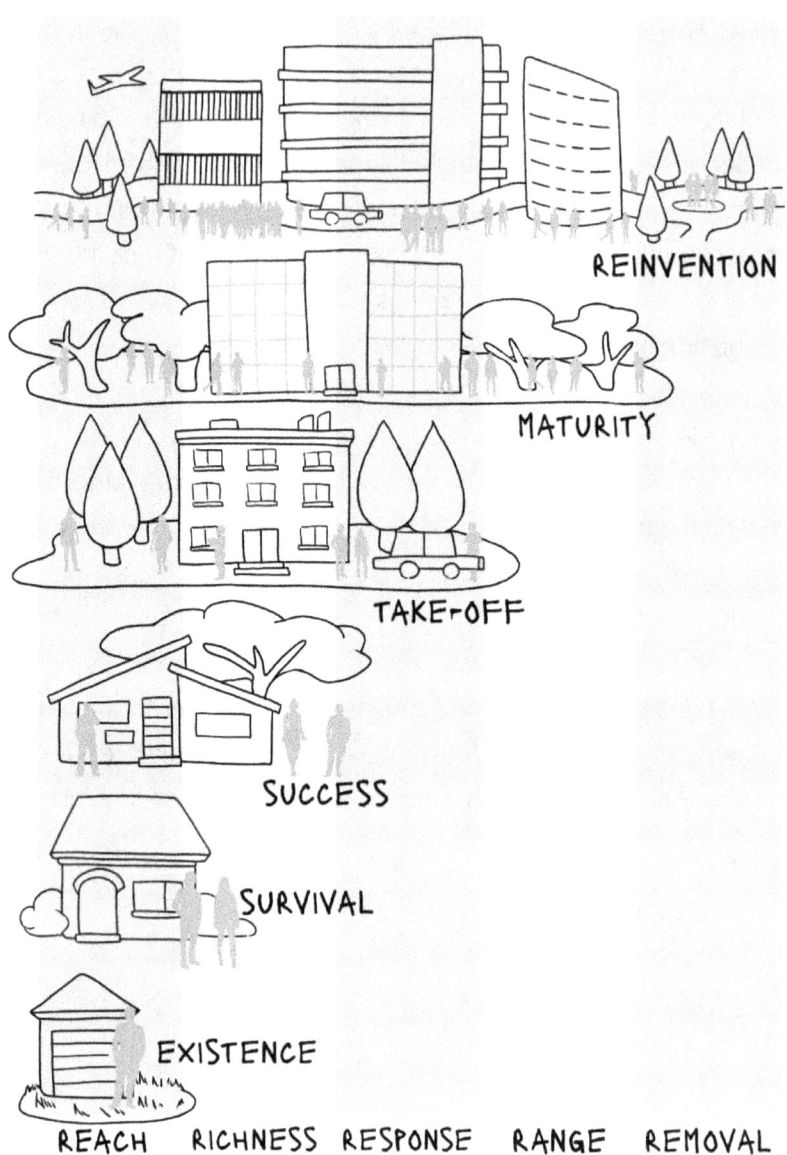

STAGES OF BUSINESS GROWTH

It is important to know that businesses grow through six stages.

Stage 1 - Existence

At the Existence Stage, the aim is to get customers and deliver your product or service. Critical to success is the business owner's ability to work in the business. The goals of the business and the personal goals of the owner should align. Here, a firm may not yet have made any real profit. It is best to adopt technologies that help the business **reach** more customers.

Stage 2 - Survival

At the Survival Stage, the aim is to cover overheads and break even. The business owner's ability to work in the business remains vital. The business needs access to resources and cash. It must decide how big and fast it wants to grow. Cultivating a strategic mindset is helpful. Selene first came to me at this stage. Here, it is best to adopt technologies that help **reach** more customers and additional suppliers.

Stage 3 - Success

At the Success Stage, the aim should be to grow, sell or merge the business. There should be a focus on the quality of people and strategic planning. Here the tired yet successful owner will do well to increase the quality of the people on the bus. Regular use of strategy notes will help. It is best to adopt technologies that help with **reach** and **richness**. Rich data about the business, employee performances and the marketplace will assist with strategic planning.

Stage 4 – Take-off

At the Take-off Stage, the aim is to grow rapidly and sustainably. The focus should remain on the quality of people and strategic planning. The successful owner must delegate well and demand that systems and operational plans be created. Repeated use of strategy notes will help. Paul first came to me at this stage. As with earlier stages, it is helpful to have technologies that address **reach and richness**. Adding technologies that help with **response** can provide real-time updates around production efficiency, supply chain logistics and customer experiences.

Stage 5 - Maturity

At the Maturity Stage, the aim is to increase control while staying entrepreneurial and perhaps groom the business for sale. Detailed strategic and operational plans are needed. Board members need to master the Strategic Mindset Process, and leaders will benefit from the repeated use of strategy notes. As before, it is helpful to have technologies that address **reach**, **richness** and **response**. Adding technologies that give suppliers, employees and customers access to a **range** of business metrics, at the push of a button, is critical.

STEP FIVE: GROW DIGITAL WINGS

Stage 6 – Reinvention

The final stage of business growth is Reinvention. This stage is often triggered by a threat to the existing business. Here the focus is one of conserving funds and staying entrepreneurial. Your product or service may be nearing the end of its useful life. This is a paradoxical stage where, despite past successes, many businesses fail. To succeed, it is critical to eliminate unprofitable activities, fail often and learn fast, and attempt to self-cannibalize your best offerings before a competitor does. At this stage, technologies that assist with **reach**, **richness**, **response** and **range** continue to be helpful. However, to remain lean and agile, new technologies that support the **removal** of people, pain and processes from the business will be critical. If removal is done well, the business can move to a new beginning.

Many businesses at the Maturity Stage that scale back or file for bankruptcy manage to stay alive and re-enter the game at the Existence Stage. For some companies, reinvention is not possible. Enron, Arthur Anderson and Lehman Brothers were not given a second chance. Other companies that filed for bankruptcy like GM, Marvel and Texaco, re-invented themselves. Apple went from Maturity to Re-invention to Existence. In 1997, Apple was on the verge of going bust when Bill Gates swooped in with an investment that allowed Apple to continue to exist[28]. Apple then completed all six stages of business growth once more, reaching Maturity in 2000, with the release of the iPod. Apple learned well.

Today, Apple conserves funds and stays entrepreneurial. It has technologies in place to help it with reach, richness, response, range and removal. Apple eliminated unprofitable activities. It removed its problematic dealer network and, more recently, its overreliance on Chinese manufacturing. It keeps self-cannibalizing its best products before a competitor does. Apple is also choosing to protect its flanks and cannibalize its brand a little. In 2020, Apple staged its cheapest phone ever, the iPhone SE 2020.

In using the six stages of business growth, you will see that selling or merging your business at the Success and Maturity stages can be worthwhile end games. Knowing this can help you allocate your time, energy and resources more effectively. The selling price of your business should take into account the value the business will likely generate in the future, rather than the all too common mistake of recovering only the cash historically invested, topped up with some desired margin[29].

Automating your business with technology should be incremental and continuous[30]. It is quite common for businesses at the earlier stages of growth to adopt response and removal technologies before they embrace richness and range. For example, a solo business, might open their doors at the Existence Stage, with fast response smart-pay devices that remove the need for cash and cashiers. It is essential to consider the role of new technology and customer needs to improve reach, richness, response, range and removal at appropriate stages of growth. This way, you are never left behind. You are ready to take full advantage of new AI and automation applications as they emerge.

ACTIVITY FIVE
GROW DIGITAL WINGS

Two-thirds of the way down the one-page strategy note, prioritize your ongoing commitment to growing digital wings. The discipline of replacing legacy systems with more functional and enabling systems can be supported in this part of your strategy note. For a new player, a good way is to start with small commitments to leading-edge technologies and then reassess. The key is to make sure new technologies gradually add value in terms of reach, richness, response, range and removal.

1. What internet technology could leverage customer and supplier reach for your business? Like Microsoft, how could you move your product or service towards a digitally enabled annual subscription that provides a recurring revenue base?

2. What algorithms and big data sets could give you richer information for decision making?

3. Which mobile apps could help you respond quicker within and outside your business?

4. What integrated database solutions could bring your full range of management functions and reporting processes together?

5. What advanced cognition and robotic systems could remove costly people, pain and processes from your business?

It's time to write out a short statement about your ongoing commitment to growing digital wings. What technologies are you currently bringing into the business? In a sentence or two, name the technologies and how they add value. If you are not presently adopting a new aspect of technology into the business, consider the technologies that might best support the implementation of your current recommendation.

The strategy note must record your ongoing commitment to digitally advancing your business in some way. Once you have recorded your current or next technology commitment, revisit your recommendation.

Is it still appropriate? Should you modify it, in light of the digital wings you are committed to growing?

If needed, update your recommendation now.

STEP FIVE: GROW DIGITAL WINGS

```
STRATEGY NOTE - JUNE QUARTER

1. RECOMMENDATION

2. DEBT SCORE   QUICK SCORE   LEADER SCORE   TRIBE SCORE

3. ANALYSIS




4. OPTIONS




5. DIGITAL WINGS
```

"In a global, digital economy, if information technology is not a strategic asset, it's a strategic liability."

Peter Weill

TASK SIX

ALIGN YOUR ACTIONS

THE STRATEGY NOTE

TASK SIX
ALIGN YOUR ACTIONS

How will you deliver on your recommendation?

A series of action steps that align with your recommendation are needed.

If you have ever rowed a boat, you will appreciate that traveling in a straight line is impossible. Keeping the boat level, applying the same force on each oar, and making sure your blades enter and exit the water at the same time helps. Yet, international rowing events are won and lost by race margins of 2cm over a 2km course. Often, the difference between gold and silver medal crews is not fitness or strength, but how well they align their actions and correct their course. The same alignment and corrections are needed for your business.

During a long-haul flight, if a plane's left-wing tilts down a fraction of a degree for a few seconds, it could alter the final destination by hundreds of miles. This is why the entire journey is calculated ahead of time, based on projected winds, and each individual airspace's route requirements. If the pilot wants to make a change to their wing-tilt, heading, speed, altitude or route, they must first seek approval from air traffic control.

TASK SIX: ALIGN YOUR ACTIONS

A well-aligned business also requires planning ahead of time, but with small adjustments to the firm's strategic orientation, often at the edges. Businesses create new capabilities, eliminate old ones, raise the quality of some services, and reduce others. Significant changes to policy require approval from the business owner and updated recommendations.

One day soon, AI and automation will seamlessly control all inflight changes and make firmwide recommendations in real time.

UNITED BREAKS GUITARS

In the highly competitive airline industry, airline companies regularly align their strategy with shifts in consumer price sensitivity. For example, reducing service quality can deliver cost savings and increased profits. In the long term, cost cutting can provide substantial financial gains or result in over-efficiencies that destroy value, reputation and safety. In 2008, musician Dave Carroll and his band flew from Halifax to Nebraska. During a layover in Chicago, Carroll discovered that baggage handlers under pressure had been throwing guitar cases with little or no care. As a result, Carroll's $3,500 Taylor guitar was severely damaged[31]. After nine months of fruitless negotiations with United, Carroll wrote a song entitled 'United Breaks Guitars.' He recorded a YouTube video that went viral[32], attracting 150,000 views on its first day.

Today the video has close to 20M views. Industry commentators noted that within a month of the video's release, United Airlines' stock price fell 10%, potentially costing stockholders $180M. A few years back, it appears that United Airlines had adopted a strategy that raised the passenger quota of its flights to beyond capacity. When there was the usual flurry of last-minute cancellations, their aircraft would still have a nearly full manifest. If the flight numbers spilled over, passengers were offered financial incentives to disembark and take the next flight. This strategy backfired in April 2017, when UA Flight 3411 reached overcapacity, without any passengers willing to disembark. Despite doubling the $400 incentive to $800, security officials forcibly dragged Dr. David Dao from the plane[33].

In the process, Dao suffered a concussion, a broken nose, and lost two teeth. A poll conducted three days after the incident revealed vital data. United customers' noses had been put out of joint. Seventy-nine percent of prospective fliers who had heard of the event said they would choose a non-United Airlines flight. A further forty-four percent said they would prefer a non-United Airlines flight, even if it cost an additional US$66 and took an extra three hours. Whenever you reduce or raise anything, there can be benefits, and there are risks. The same is true when you deliberately create or eliminate some aspects of your business. Significant changes are inherently risky. Yet, even small changes carry risks.

Change not aligned with your Claim to Fame can be dangerous.

TASK SIX: ALIGN YOUR ACTIONS

CLAIM TO FAME

Whenever you create, raise, reduce or eliminate something in your business, make sure it aligns with your Claim to Fame and your core reason for being. United Airlines' Claim to Fame is 'Connecting People and Uniting the World.' Throwing guitars around the tarmac and maiming innocent passengers revealed a lack of alignment between strategy, policy and action. If your next steps contradict your core principles, then those actions are not aligned.

You may not always get alignment right. Failure can provide a step towards better alignment next time. Kimberly Clark's Claim to Fame was once milling paper. Today they make consumer goods. Today Apple makes wearable mini iPads called Apple Watches. Staying aligned with your Claim to Fame and being prepared to move from an industry approach to a market approach helps you stay relevant.

As the marketplace around you changes, you may need to change too. Uber's Claim to Fame is in passenger logistics and rostering shift workers. Apple's is in smart devices. Kimberly Clark's is in disposable paper and plastics. Coca-Cola's is in global snack food and drink distribution. Had United Airlines' become violating passengers and their luggage? If a business does not consistently align execution with strategy and ethics, their Claim to Fame can drift into infamous territory.

A shadow Claim to Fame can hurt your brand. Both Apple and Nike are infamous for exploiting illegal child labor in China and other third-world countries. A shadow Claim to Fame can be used intentionally. Harley Davidson knows it can't match BMW, Suzuki, Honda or Ducati in motorcycle safety, performance, fuel efficiency or design. However, they maximized their reputation for having a huge, loud and chrome-covered motorbike. At one point, Harley Davidson made up ground[34] by suggesting their Claim to Fame was, "Selling 43-year-old accountants the ability to dress in leather, ride through small towns and have people be afraid of them!" Knowing your Claim to Fame helps ensure that your recommendation and action steps are aligned. Changing lanes from time to time can make sense, but always keep your Claim to Fame in view.

On the pages that follow, write your Claim to Fame.

NEXT STEPS

The sixth task in the strategy note is to align your future actions and write them out as steps. Your strategy note is bound by time. Your recommendation will become less relevant as time passes. Your goal is to come up with the three most important steps your business must execute to implement your recommendation. To help create your three steps, jot down three headings, People, Places, and Things. Under each heading, consider the kinds of steps you could take. Here are some examples.

TASK SIX: ALIGN YOUR ACTIONS

People

Step 1. Raise the quality of our hiring process to help our front-line managers get the best people working on our projects sooner. Before acting, take a baseline % staff turnover rate and assess future results against this.

Places

Step 2. Reduce our overreliance on China for sourcing and find other countries to secure parts and manufacturing. Before acting, record product quality and inventory turnover rates for existing components and assess future results against these.

Things

Step 3. Create a secure server offsite with a mirror image of our daily backup to eliminate our reliance on the internet and the cloud for our secure data storage. Carry out a zero-tolerance risk assessment for all current and proposed storage options as well as a cost-benefit analysis of both.

Your three steps could relate to people or be any combination of people, places and things. Once you have decided on your three steps, you should visit the question of risk. Action steps that do not align with your Claim to Fame are risky. United Airlines' passenger removal policy showed us what can happen. Even action steps aligned with your Claim to Fame and your written recommendation can still be risky. No action is ever risk-free. Also, doing nothing carries a risk.

United hoped that by doing nothing and ignoring Dave Carroll, he would eventually go away. You may not be in the airline business. However, a risk assessment of your approach is still needed.

As you finalize your three steps, carry out a risk assessment. For each of your three action steps, ask seven questions:

1. Strategic Risk: Will this action weaken the business in any way?
2. Compliance Risk: Will upcoming regulations negate this action?
3. Operational Risk: Will this action add dangers or complexity?
4. Financial Risk: Will there be hidden costs with this action?
5. Reputational Risk: Do ethical dilemmas accompany this action?
6. Political Risk: Will a change of government neutralize this action?
7. Market Risk: Will market fluctuations thwart this action?

The greatest risk of all is a lack of action. The third and final lesson I took from TJ is that most companies don't fail from a lack of talent or strategic vision, but they fail from a lack of execution and action. Inaction negates learning. Inaction is a signal that confirmation bias, entropy and inertia have set in. A firm that fails to execute, will be executed. The Strategy Note's discipline of writing out your recommendation and your three action steps prompts your business to keep learning by regularly executing strategy. And, this learning ensures your business survives and thrives.

TASK SIX: ALIGN YOUR ACTIONS

ACTIVITY SIX
ALIGN YOUR ACTIONS

Four-fifths of the way down your strategy note, write your three action steps. An excellent way to begin this task is to write a sentence such as:

'These next steps deliver on the recommendation and align with our Claim to Fame of {insert your Claim to Fame}'

We're nearly done. Your strategy note is almost complete.

Write your three steps in a way that raises the awareness of risks and offers ways to mitigate them. With risk mitigation included, here is an example of three action steps.

Step 1. Raise the quality of our hiring process to help our front-line managers get the best people working on our projects sooner. Before acting, take a baseline % staff turnover rate and assess future results against this. Evaluate the impact of industrial relations laws an incoming conservative government may introduce next year.

Step 2. Reduce our overreliance on China for sourcing and find other countries to secure parts and manufacturing. Before acting, record product quality and inventory turnover rates for existing components and assess future results against these. Understand relevant foreign exchange patterns and tariffs. Assess possible price retaliation moves by China.

Step 3. Create a secure server offsite with a mirror image of our daily backup to eliminate our reliance on the internet and the Cloud for our secure data storage. Carry out a zero-tolerance risk assessment for all current and proposed storage options as well as a cost-benefit analysis of both. Raise our data protection to asymmetric standards with 2048-bit key dual encryption.

It's time to write. Four-fifths of the way down the one-page strategy note, write your claim to fame and your three steps with risk mitigation included.

Once done, revisit your recommendation at the top of the strategy note.

Is it still appropriate?

Great.

TASK SIX: ALIGN YOUR ACTIONS

STRATEGY NOTE — JUNE QUARTER

1. RECOMMENDATION

2. DEBT SCORE   QUICK SCORE   LEADER SCORE   TRIBE SCORE

3. ANALYSIS

4. OPTIONS

5. DIGITAL WINGS

6. NEXT STEPS

"If you want to go fast, go alone. If you want to go far, go together."

African Proverb

CONCLUSION

There is no finish line.

The world of business, technology, people and ethical considerations keep evolving. Sometimes businesses succeed and other times they die from pandemic like setbacks.

As human beings, we get to create our future and our ending. Inside, we have a finish line. We can stop running at any time or keep moving. The choice is ours. The real value in challenging yourself is to test the limits of your human values and spirit. The ethical values that drive your business will help it survive. The spirit with which you keep executing strategy will ensure it thrives. Companies like Uber and Apple embody this spirit. Today both firms enjoy evolved leadership, entrepreneurial spirit, and a unique ability to execute strategy.

How about you?

Your life is an adventure. If you own or lead a business, you have already answered the call to grow something bigger, better, bolder and brighter. To keep answering the call, better questions will be needed. The right questions ensure your business ladder is resting against the right wall. We have been living through a period with record debt levels and inflated company valuations. With advancing digital disruption and the cost competition it brings, innovation is needed more than ever. When the going gets tough, it is important to get going. The use of strategy notes can give your business the momentum it needs. Being smarter is also important. Cultivating the leadership discipline of the strategy note helps you maintain a strategic mindset and digitally advance your business.

You can ensure your business remains hearty and fit by being aware of your debt to equity and quick ratios. Today, many employees are seeking greater meaning from their work, and leaders have to demonstrate higher levels of emotional intelligence. Reporting the level of trust in your humble leaders, as well as their increasing measures of faith in your people will help your business remain healthy. Carrying out regular market and customer analysis will help you formulate worthwhile future recommendations.

Creating future scenarios and listening seriously to stories about disaster will keep your business alive. Using proven strategy tools and drawing decision trees can help you name and choose options. The technologies you used to build your business need replacing or upgrading to keep growing digital wings. Keeping your Claim to Fame in mind will help. Have your Claim to Fame close whenever you review strategy, consider new markets, alter your capabilities, change policies, or act on recommendations.

Unless, your plan is to 'uber it.'

CONCLUSION

'UBER IT'

To 'uber' something means to exceed the expected limits. As a company, Uber periodically challenges and changes its Claim to Fame, by testing the boundaries of what's possible. Uber personifies the six tasks that make up a strategy note. Uber updates their strategic recommendations regularly. Uber has a debt to equity ratio of just 0.1 and a healthy quick ratio of 2.0. Uber has a highly talented, credible, and diverse board and executive team of men and women that engender high levels of trust and instill faith in their people. Uber keeps tuning into the consumer marketplace, rather than being narrowly defined by one industry. Uber embraces and names new options. Uber commits to growing digital wings by leveraging new technology quickly. Uber's next steps keep them one step ahead. They 'ignite opportunity by setting the world in motion.'

Recently, Giorgio Alessi became the first 'Uberman' by completing the world's most challenging ultra-triathlon. Alessi offers us an inspiring reminder of our own vast and untapped potential. The Uberman event includes a cycle leg equal to five stages of the Tour de France and a running leg equivalent to five marathons. The running leg travels up the highest peak and across the hottest desert in the United States. The event starts with a thirty-four-kilometer swim stage from Catalina Island to Palos Verdes - a grueling ocean course filled with strong currents, tankers, cruise ships, sharks and jellyfish.

The ocean your ship sails upon is not always friendly. A strong balance sheet, a healthy crew and a clear direction are needed to weather the storm. When Steve Jobs regained the helm at Apple, the firm was sinking. Steve threw man after man overboard, to reduce cost and avoid disaster. When Bill Gates threw Steve a financial lifeline, Steve was able to hire talented people, like Tim Cook, and chart a new course.

As your business recovers from any setback, remember the revealed traits of your leaders during a crisis. Kindly move the wrong people off the bus and the right people onto the bus and into the right seats. In the beginning, Uber had some pretty unsavory leaders[35]. Today their bus and future look much healthier. Both Apple and Uber are future-focused and here for the long run. They generate options and stick to their lane, unless they see an unfulfilled market they can meet well with new technology. By leading strategy effectively, Apple and Uber remain outside the 96% of businesses that fail inside a decade.

END GAMES

Every business needs an end game. You set yourself up for a worthwhile end game by practicing things that embody your passion and purpose and add value to the world. Right understanding offers you a pathway to right action. Strategy notes help you to practice the linking of understanding, relationship and action. In the end, do you want to be remembered for growing a bigger, better, brighter and bolder business?

CONCLUSION

Twenty-three years ago, I read a note entitled No Excuses Management by TJ Rogers. TJ Rogers founded Cypress Semiconductors in 1982 and stepped down as CEO in 2016. Since then, TJ has remained active on the sidelines to ensure the successful sale of the company and a highly rewarding end game. April 2020 marked the end of independence for Cypress Semiconductors. German firm Infineon brought Cypress for $9B. An impressive sale, resulting in a price to earnings ratio of 25:1. TJ's sustained success and end game result in the notoriously cut-throat semiconductor industry has been a fantastic feat.

TJ taught me that companies don't fail from a lack of talent or strategic vision, but they fail from a lack of execution and action. He also revealed that strategic plans are often obsolete within hours or days of being written. Finally, TJ taught me that during prosperous times, danger lurks for every business. Growth masks waste, extravagance, and inefficiency. I have attempted to address the three lessons I took from TJ in the creation of The Strategy Note.

The pandemic provided lessons too. During the Coronavirus lockdowns, it was astonishing to see the recovery and regeneration of ecosystems in our communities, alongside the tragic end to tens of millions of human lives. We re-entered the world with a renewed awareness of our collective footprint and a new mass extinction scenario for our entire species. Like Greta Thunberg, millions of people stopped flying during the pandemic and our planet echoed 'thank you.' Could your business reverse the order of its traditional priorities of profit, people and then planet to planet, people and then profit? With each precious sunset, we can reflect on our day and write out the adventure we want to create for our businesses and the planet for years to come.

GAME ON

One morning, after fifteen years, Selene returned for more advice. She had a mature business and a healthy retirement in place. Andrew, Selene's business partner, had offered to buy her out for less than Selene had wanted.

I said to myself, 'Game on.'

I asked Selene, "If I could grant you anything you wanted, what would it be?"

Selene smiled and thought for a moment.

Selene replied, "I need a new adventure. I want to exit this business, but for four times what my partner is offering."

After working with Selene to develop her new strategy note and hone her negotiation skills, she was able to enter into constructive discussions with Andrew. This resulted in the sale of her shares, at the value she was seeking.

CONCLUSION

I was happy to help Selene receive greater value, in return for the popular body-safe and planet-saving products she had been creating for twenty years.

With a heart-filled smile, Selene thanked me and headed out. There was a happy tear in my eye.

From her iPhone, Selene requested an Uber.

Selene was off and running to her next adventure.

How will you create the next adventure for your business, your people and the planet using The Strategy Note?

EPILOGUE
THE NEXT LEVEL

EXISTENTIAL FLEXIBILITY

I wrote this epilogue two years after first publishing The Strategy Note.

Recently, my daughter Lauren, who created the illustrations for The Strategy Note, called me late one rain-filled afternoon on her commute home. Lauren was distressed because her car had stalled on a rising section of a two-lane tunnel inside a city bypass. By the time I arrived on the scene, traffic was banked up for miles, with cars and trucks forced to merge into one lane.

Before heading to the scene, Lauren sent me her location pin. As I contemplated the task at hand, I realised driving, hailing a taxi or booking an Uber, as she suggested, would be an hour-long exercise. Lauren was six miles away, and gridlock was setting in.

As The Strategy Guy, my task, much of the time, is to think 'outside the box'. In these moments, I utilise existential flexibility. Existential flexibility reduces a problem to its essence and requires imagination to craft options. Existential flexibility requires us to start without knowing how our strategy will ultimately play out. In reducing a problem to its essence, we need to keep sight of our purpose and identify the few critical success factors we must perform well on.

Making sure Lauren was safe inside the tunnel was the first critical success factor. Over the phone, I made sure she was safe. The next critical success factor was to assist her. I realised roadside assist services would be peak hour and wet weather impacted, and they could be an hour away if called. A related success factor was to get on the scene quickly to support her.

I reached inside the hallway cupboard and scooped up my moto keys and rider helmet, and headed quickly for my sports bike - a handy option. With city-wide traffic at its 5 pm crawl, my lane-splitting in the wet went smoothly and swiftly. Fifteen minutes later, I parked adjacent to the gently rising tunnel and walked inside.

After a reassuring hug, I popped Lauren into the driver's seat of her small car, and with most of my strength, I started pushing her up the rise. My first efforts were challenging. The car roll forwards a little and then back. I tried again - the same result. I pushed again and kept the pressure on. The car rolled a little further, and then the soles of my shoes slipped on the greasy road. I chose to keep pushing. I bent my knees and repositioned my feet, and kept pushing. Slowly, slowly Lauren's car rolled forward and kept moving. But only if I was disciplined and kept my 'shoulder to the wheel'.

I did not let up.

Then something predictable happened.

From behind me, two guys appeared. They had decided to park their cars in the lane directly behind us and make the task of pushing uphill easy. I shifted positions and ran up alongside the car to ensure Lauren's brakes still worked. The car was moving quickly and reaching the top of the hill near the tunnel exit.

Later Lauren shared that some slowly passing motorists called out to her during the fifteen minutes she waited for me to arrive. She shared that two Irish ladies asked her if someone was coming, and a young bearded motorist yelled out, "Life sucks for you!"

When the two guys behind saw that I had the rain-drenched purpose of getting Lauren's car up the rise, they joined in. A successful business is not that different. When a leader continually pursues a worthy goal (clearing a blocked traffic lane) and persists with it, others notice the progress, even if that initial progress is small, and help.

Atop the rise was a downhill stretch, and once there, I thanked the two guys for helping. I then jumped into the car (manual gearbox) and showed Lauren how to complete a hill start. With her car engine running, I returned for my moto and followed her safely home.

Getting a stalled engine or a new business moving requires the application of a significant initial force to get things going and then the consistent application of force to keep things going. Pushing a car uphill and turning a business flywheel are similar feats.

Most businesses that get their flywheel moving still falter. Some falter because their chosen terrain is too steep. Others falter because they never apply enough initial force to be viable and valuable. An established business that fails inside a decade may have lost its way. That business may have stopped applying the force and direction needed for momentum and long term success.

EPILOGUE: THE NEXT LEVEL

Since first publishing The Strategy Note, I have worked with multiple groups every month to craft, review and update strategy notes for their businesses. With three of my clients, they hoped the monthly strategy note review process would automatically future proof their business. I discovered with these clients that the strategy note increased their focus, motivation, and accountability. What it did not do so well was reinforce their business model.

All businesses need a business model that articulates how that business will make money and scale. With the majority of my clients, their leaders could say how their business made money and name the activities they needed to work on consistently to scale the business. However with my other three mentioned clients, getting clear on their strategic approach required extra work, and once done, they wanted to fit their business model into the strategy note.

Eventually, we found by trial and error that listing the four to six components of their business flywheel in the strategy note, just after their health scores, was helpful. I have recorded these next level ideas here, to help evolving businesses to play a bigger game.

PLAY A BIGGER GAME

The flywheel idea is the work of Jim Collins, and it elegantly addresses the question of your business model. Before introducing Jim's flywheel idea, I'd like to talk about what sort of game your business or organisation plays.

THE STRATEGY NOTE

Are you playing a finite game?

A finite game is one where there are winners and losers, and beating the competition is essential. Former CEO of GE, Jack Welch, was a master of the finite game. Jack told his leaders that GE should only play in markets where they could be number one or number two in market share. Once GE slipped to fourth in any market, Jack made sure GE exited.

Jack understood that firms with dominant market shares benefited financially by increasing returns from scale. In other words, the bigger you are, the lower your variable production and unit distribution costs will be. This is due to the substantial scale efficiencies that come from being number one or number two. Also, the proportion of fixed expenses or overheads as a percentage of costs are much lower if you are big.

Playing finite game after finite game, if you transition quickly, can allow you to become big and rich. However, it can also be exhausting and even soul-destroying. Relentless opportunism without making sure one's firm has a profound longer-term mission or superordinate goal are the hallmarks of perpetual finite game players.

Maybe you are playing an infinite game?

Playing the infinite game is something popular presenter Simon Sinek often shares with his audiences. Simon shares that Microsoft's secret and not so secret ambition was to beat Apple. On the other hand, Apple had no interest in competing with anyone except itself.

EPILOGUE: THE NEXT LEVEL

Apple focuses relentlessly on bringing the best user experience possible to its customers through its innovative hardware, software, and services.

So, back to your business.

Will your firm outlive you?

Will the value your business creates have a positive impact on future generations?

Will your firm eventually change this world for the better?

If so, then it's likely you are an infinite game player.

On the other hand, your business focus may make you a finite player. Your firm may meet a short term or transitory need with no long term impact. Like Jack, your business may win again and again by leveraging a stream of untapped short term economic opportunities.

At an existential level, the games of life and business are infinite. Existence allows us to play with infinite and finite mindsets. Understanding which way your business plays the game is essential. Players with an infinite approach move slower and more consistently. They are patient, disciplined and remain focused on an extended or infinite game. Players who adopt a finite approach prioritise issues like budgets, deadlines, profits and competition.

As we move to examine a flywheel for your business, knowing the type of player you are will help determine which four to six components should make up your flywheel.

As a father of four, I have gradually become an infinite player.

My future may include finding ways to keep my daughter safe and get her car moving. It will also mean repeatedly role-playing a depressed patient to help another daughter practice the suicide prevention protocol she is learning in psychology at university. On other days, for a third daughter, it is inspecting houses she and her partner are considering buying. Or with my son, it means ninety minutes of catching and shooting basketballs hurled at us from a Dr Dish Basketball Shooting Machine. One day, I'll be a grandfather, and the infinite game of loving my expanding family will continue.

As a motivational speaker and strategic advisor, I also play an infinite game. My purpose is to help groups and individuals create brighter futures, with my talks, books, courses and consulting work. To help play the game, I have a six-component flywheel for my business, which appears below.

In the centre of the flywheel is my purpose. If you create a flywheel for your firm, your flywheel's centre is a handy place to write your purpose, mission or claim to fame.

At various points around my flywheel are six components or activities. If I action these six consistently, my flywheel will turn faster and create the momentum needed to fulfil my purpose and generate the income to support myself, my family and the at-need groups I assist.

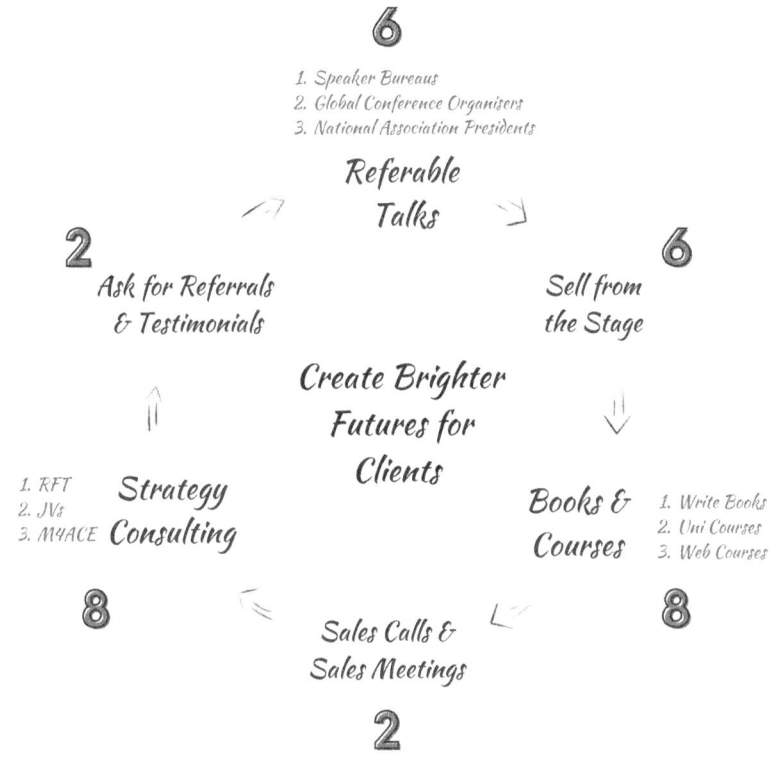

Three of my six components are primary support activities. Selling from the Stage, Sales Calls and Asking for Referrals do not add much value or generate income in their own right. The other three components do. These are delivering Referable Talks, Books and Courses, and Strategy Consulting. When I am busy with these three direct income activities, the other three activities can suffer.

So what happens?

I don't make time to write books and courses. I don't have time to schedule sales calls. I forget to ask for referrals. When this happens, gradually, my flywheel starts to decelerate, and my business moves slower.

To keep my flywheel moving, I do two things.

Firstly, I add secondary support activities that feed into one or more of my six components. Often, these secondary support activities benefit from AI and automation. For example, I utilise a Grammarly subscription to check my prose and spelling when writing books or courses. Having my motivational speaker information on multiple speaker bureau websites and global speaker search engines creates bookings I would not have had on my own. My Monday.com subscription helps organise my sales and automatically score my CRM performance.

The second thing I do to keep my flywheel moving is to score my recent activity level on each of the six components. For example, at the time of writing, I have just written a university-based strategy course for accountants, updated two strategy books, booked a three-state speaking roadshow and am about to run four offsite strategy retreats. So right now, my scores for writing, consulting, talks and selling from the stage are above five out of ten. However, sales activity and referrals are about two out of ten and need my attention, or my business will slow down later in the year.

CREATE YOUR FLYWHEEL

The best way to create your flywheel is to buy a copy of Jim Collins' book, *The Flywheel*, and complete its exercises. To create a working flywheel, Jim typically facilitates offsite strategy retreats with his clients, the likes of which include Amazon, Vanguard and Intel.

In essence, the rules for creating the first version of your flywheel are as follows.

1. Limit your flywheel to four, five or six components that form a progressing cyclical sequence that helps your firm add value, make money and scale.

2. Consistent performance by any single component on its own should move your flywheel faster in a clockwise direction.

3. The output from each component should be a catalyst or compelling input for the flywheel component that follows it.

To increase momentum in your business, you may like to take your strategy note to the next level, by creating a flywheel for your business and then scoring your flywheel's components each time you update your strategy note.

As with any decision process, garbage-in-gabage-out can happen. The strategy note is not immune to this. The strategy note will keep you focused and accountable. A business can be like Jack in the old fable, who climbed a giant beanstalk. Scaling a giant beanstalk or a massive ladder requires focus and commitment. However, if your beanstalk is poking through the wrong cloud or your ladder is resting against the wrong wall, your business will grind to a halt or even go in the reverse direction.

Whether you are playing a finite game or an infinite game, creating a flywheel and including its components' scores in your strategy note, will help ensure your ladder is resting against the right wall.

Now you can be confident that you are regularly holding yourself accountable for doing the right things.

STRATEGY NOTE - JUNE QUARTER

1. RECOMMENDATION

2. DEBT SCORE   QUICK SCORE   LEADER SCORE   TRIBE SCORE

2.5. FLYWHEEL SCORES

TALKS	STAGE	WRITE	CALLS	CONSULT	REFER
6	6	8	2	8	2

3. ANALYSIS

4. OPTIONS

5. DIGITAL WINGS

6. NEXT STEPS

*"Greatness is primarily not a function of circumstance.
Greatness, it turns out, is primarily a matter
of conscious choice and discipline."*

Jim Collins

APPENDIX A

INDUSTRY ATTRACTIVENESS

In the 1970s, Michael Porter studied hundreds of businesses. Porter realized that over time industry attractiveness changes and with those changes, so does industry profitability. Porter showed the attractiveness of any industry could be determined by examining six industry forces[36]. The sum of customer power, supplier power, threat of new entrants, threat of substitutes, degree of rivalry and complementary player effects reveal the likely profitability of an industry.

You can use Michael Porter's model to analyze the ongoing profitability of your industry. On the blank pages opposite, write down a description of your industry. For example, Legal Services, Cloud Computing, Real Estate, Domestic Robotics, Retail Fashion, Beauty, Hospitality, Homewares, Software Development, Health, Mining, Education or Microchip Manufacturing.

THE STRATEGY NOTE

1. Jot down the customers or clients that regularly buy from your industry. For example, European consumers represent one-tenth of the world population. Yet, they account for one-third of sales in the Global Haircare Industry. Decide if the bargaining power of customers (Customer Power) is low, moderate, or high.

2. Make a list of the significant suppliers to your industry. For example, the Hospitality Industry may rely on suppliers of retail spaces, chefs, baristas, insurance, equipment, food, beverages and coffee. Decide if the bargaining power of suppliers (Supplier Power) is low, moderate, or high.

3. Assess the threat of new entrants to your industry by jotting down their likely barriers to entry. Examples include high capital requirements for entry to the industry; existing customers' perceived costs of switching their purchasing to a new entrant; government policies; existing intellectual property (IP) and the threat of retaliation by incumbents, such as yourself. Decide if the Threat of New Entrants is low, moderate, or high.

    For a new entrant, speed and influence is also critical. As a new entrant, Uber quickly broke through significant barriers to entry. Barriers that Lyft, a profitable fast follower, did not have to navigate. Nevertheless, the positive brand recognition Uber attracted as a bold and trusted player, gave it credibility as it moved into other markets.

4. Make a list of products and services that are substitutes for what you produce. For example, in the automotive industry, the list of

APPENDIX A: INDUSTRY ATTRACTIVENESS

possible substitutes includes public transport, Uber rideshare, scooters and bicycles. Decide if the Threat of Substitutes is low, moderate, or high.

5. Make a list of rival players who compete against you and each other for customers and market share. Decide if the Degree of Rivalry in your industry is low, moderate, or high.

6. Consider related industries. Complementary players are firms in nearby industries with activities that complement your industry. For example, when large firms behave unethically, they get sued more often. This results in increased litigation activity which, in turn, benefits the legal profession. Decide if the Benefits from Complementary Players in your industry are low, moderate, or high.

Some industries are attractive and profitable. For example, dentists enjoy 20% profit margins with friendly trade winds. For dentists, Customer Power, Threat of Substitutes, Threat of New Entrants, Degree of Rivalry are all low, with Supplier Power being high and Benefits from Complementary Players being moderate. Other industries are less attractive. For example, under normal conditions, airlines have profit margins of around 5% with plenty of crosswinds. For airlines, Supplier Power, Customer Power, Threat of Substitutes, Threat of New Entrants and Degree of Rivalry are all moderate or high, with Benefits from Complementary Players being only moderate.

7. Review your answers and decide how attractive your industry is. Is the Overall Industry Attractiveness changing? Do you have to work harder or smarter these days to reach your customers? What is the average net profit across your industry? Where are the most favorable winds to be found? For example, software development is usually much more attractive than hardware manufacturing. Will digital innovation make your industry more or less attractive in the future and what steps can you take to take advantage of this situation?

In two or three sentences, summarize the attractiveness of your industry and any changes you expect to the six industry forces in the future. Adding this summary to your strategy note gives you and your reader a useful context for your recommendation.

APPENDIX A: INDUSTRY ATTRACTIVENESS

CUSTOMER BARGAINING POWER    SUPPLIER BARGAINING POWER

THREAT OF NEW ENTRANTS    THREAT OF SUBSTITUTES

DEGREE OF RIVALRY    BENEFITS FROM COMPLEMENTS

OVERALL INDUSTRY ATTRACTIVENESS

"The world we live in is vastly different from the world we think we live in."

Nassim Nicholas Taleb

APPENDIX B

CLAIM TO FAME

When you slow down, tune in, and do the right analysis, you can decide whether to advance, keep listening or withdraw.

Knowing your Claim to Fame helps with this decision.

Encyclopedia Britannica is a classic example of a famous business that failed to look in the rear-view mirror to see what was about to overtake them. Encyclopedia Britannica's Claim to Fame was that it was the longest-serving and most trusted general knowledge English-language encyclopedia. With advances in technology, their Claim to Fame became irrelevant. They were out of tune with their marketplace. A thirty-two-volume Encyclopedia Britannica set was selling for two-thousand dollars, at a time when digital innovation occurred in the knowledge reference industry. At that time, New Entrants were selling the same information on CD-ROM for two-hundred dollars. Today, a Substitute like Wikipedia offers one-hundred times more information for a voluntary donation, and Google Search is free.

Most of the time, your Claim to Fame will help guide your strategy and the ongoing recommendations for the business. But from time to time, your Claim to Fame should be refined.

1. Define your Claim to Fame. Your Claim to Fame could reflect your founder's vision, your business intent, 'elevator statement' or ideal customer definition. For example, the 'Big Australian' mining company BHP had founders renowned for 'thinking big'. BHP's current Claim to Fame is that it owns and operates large, long-life, low-cost, expandable, upstream assets diversified by commodity, geography, and market[37].

2. How do your customers and the marketplace perceive you? What lasting and valuable contribution does your business or firm make to the world? On the blank pages that follow, write down yours. Consider your respective competitors' Claims to Fame. How is your Claim to Fame really that different from theirs? In the end, the points of difference you identify and embody may make a world of difference.

In a sentence, write down your Claim to Fame. Adding your Claim to Fame to your strategy note will remind you and your reader of your business's unique value proposition and branding. Check your current strategy. Does it uphold your Claim to Fame? Also, check your Claim to Fame. Is it still relevant to your customers and what you need to do to remain successful?

"Being deliberately strategic about your internal capabilities enables you to create products and service options that make your customers go "Wow! I must have THAT!"

Oscar Hauptman

APPENDIX C
CRITICAL SUCCESS FACTORS

Often, there are only a handful of things a business must get right to do well. Performing brilliantly on a few things that are critical to success in your industry can help balance out some of the things that you perform poorly. Coke's ingredients such as sugar and additives do little for our health. People who reach for a Coke are looking for a wet sugary caffeine hit and a psychological feeling of being 'cool'. Coca-Cola is able to perform poorly in terms of nutrition, as long as they do well on the critical success factors for the soft drink industry.

In the soft drink industry, the factors that are most critical to success are brand recognition, country-specific printing and controlling global channels for distribution. Coca-Cola does exceptionally well at the things that are critical to success in the soft drink industry. Over time, Coca-Cola has bought out healthier snack food and soft drink players and added those brands to their powerful global distribution networks[38].

THE STRATEGY NOTE

Consider what it takes to be really successful in your industry.

For example, if you own a gym which operates in the fitness industry, you might come up with the following six critical success factors:

1. Sound financial management
2. High levels of customer service
3. Appealing workout and training spaces with modern equipment
4. Safe, social and educational training programs and classes
5. Membership pricing that aligns with a range of client preferences
6. Clean change and shower facilities

On the blank pages opposite, list the critical success factors for businesses in your industry. In a sentence or two write out the three to six most important things you must do well for your business to thrive. In a post pandemic world, what new critical success factors are key?

How well do you perform on each of these critical success factors?

Give yourself a score for each.

Including your critical success factors with corresponding performance scores in your strategy note will help to remind you and your readers of the things you must focus on to be successful. Your recommendation should be written with an awareness of your critical success factors and it may even address one of these factors specifically. Your recommendation reflects the most important thing or combination of things you should focus on right now.

APPENDIX C: CRITICAL SUCCESS FACTORS

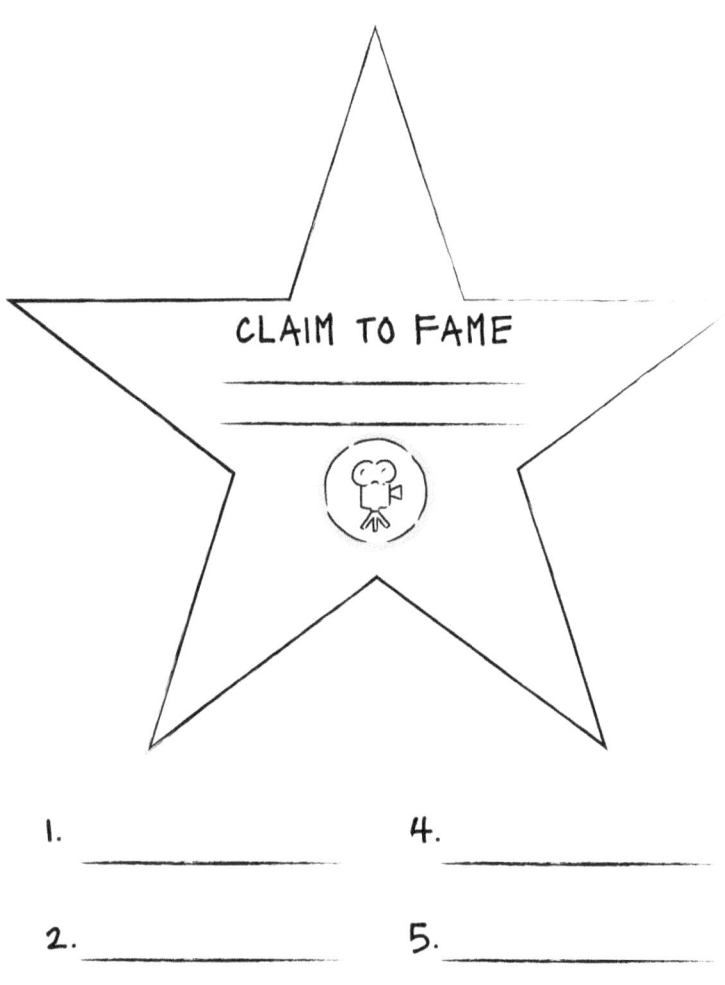

1. _____   4. _____

2. _____   5. _____

3. _____   6. _____

"There's this thing in technology, almost a disease, where the definition of success is making the most. How many clicks did you get, how many active users do you have, how many units did you sell? Everybody in technology seems to want big numbers. Steve never got carried away with that. He focused on making the best."

Tim Cook

APPENDIX D

CUSTOMER INTIMACY WHEEL

Around the time Steve Jobs returned to Apple, he had been talking with a friend and discovered that despite dozens of Apple models there was no clear answer to which computer was right for his friend. Soon thereafter, in a product meeting, Steve used what his friend taught him to help people choose an Apple Computer that was right for them[39]. Steve told his team: 'We only need to learn two answers from customers buying an Apple computer: Are you a professional user or an everyday user? Do you want your computer as a desktop or a portable?' As a result, Apple eliminated over half of its products.

Steve took the lessons learned from workspaces at Pixar. Pixar believe that, "Art is a team sport."[40] By creating centralised hubs that provided coffee and snacks, Steve ensured people stayed connected. Employees, contractors and customers had to walk through the same spaces, to attend meetings and focus groups. Apple employees and customers constantly passed ideas in passing, rather than staying locked away in individual departments. Thanks to Steve's connections, Apple transformed its level of customer intimacy from being a *Product Provider* with a network of resellers to *Selling the Benefits* directly via Apple Stores. Apple Geniuses engaged in *Two-way Relationships* with customers, which eventually led to a community of *Alliance Partners,* via its App Store and third-party add-ons.

Review the Customer Intimacy Wheel[41] on the page that follows. Consider the needs of your customers?

Do they see you as simply a *Product Provider*? If so, how might you better *Sell the Benefits*, build better *Two-way Relationships* with customers and perhaps attract complementary *Alliance Partners*?

APPENDIX D: CUSTOMER INTIMACY WHEEL

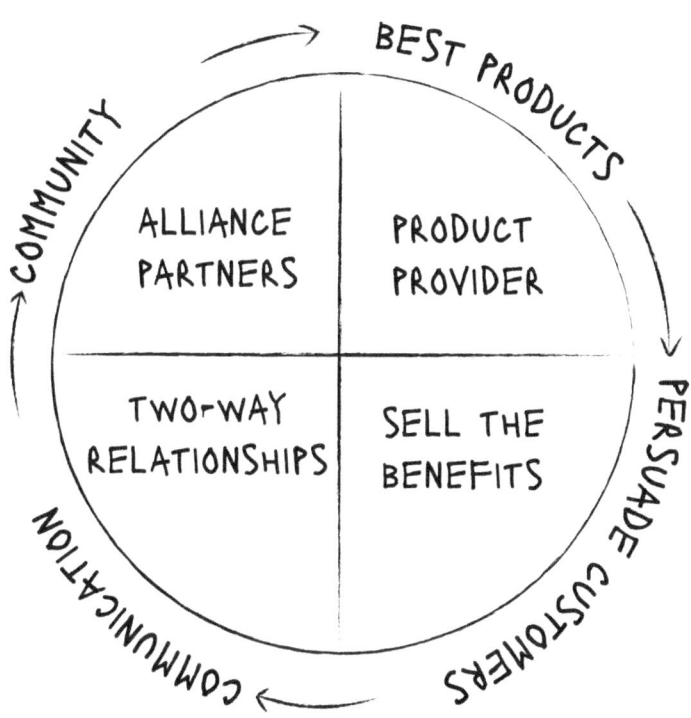

"Your most unhappy customers are your greatest source of learning."

Bill Gates

APPENDIX E

SCENARIO PLANNING

The future belongs to those businesses that see possibilities first. This usually involves Scenario Planning[42]. Appropriately done, Scenario Planning requires you to create five (5) imaginative stories about the future.

These five stories are an extension of life as you know it. Four of these stories come with a twist. Telling stories, giving them each a name and keeping the stories alive helps to build memories of them, in advance. These stories help you to understand what could lie ahead for your business. If you share the stories and their names with your entire team, your people will 'remember the future' and help you see when one, or more of these futures are beginning to materialize. This is what Bill Gates tried to do in 2015, with the scenario of a future virus.

THE STRATEGY NOTE

To create your five stories or scenarios, invite others from diverse backgrounds (e.g. science, government, economics, technology, psychology, sociology, demography) to help shape these scenarios. Include indicators and characteristics for each scenario. In time, these indicators will help confirm that a scenario is heading your way.

We are going to create:

1. The Official Future Scenario
2. A More of the Same but Much Worse Scenario
3. A More of the Same but Much Better Scenario
4. A Different and Much Worse Scenario
5. A Different and Much Better Scenario

Scenario planning heightens your awareness so that if characteristics start appearing that are associated with one of your scenarios, you sense these as markers of change. Seeing change earlier means you can start responding sooner or capitalise upon an opportunity more quickly. Here is a quick example of how to name and frame these five scenarios, from a point early on in the pandemic.

The first is the Official Future Scenario – it is the status quo, just ticking along mostly unchanged into the future. A name for this scenario could be 'She'll be right mate.'

The second is a More of the Same but Much Worse Scenario. For example, seven quarters of negative GDP growth, followed by a return to positive growth. A name for this scenario could be 'The L shaped recovery.'

APPENDIX E: SCENARIO PLANNING

The third is a More of the Same but Much Better Scenario. For example, a return to healthy living and restricted business trading within twelve months with advanced testing and mandatory quarantine for all overseas arrivals for a further six months. A name for this scenario could be 'The Kangaroo Bounce' or perhaps 'The V or W recovery.'

The fourth is a Different but Much Worse Scenario. For example, the virus eventually mutates. Bringing a more substantial second and third wave which causes us to remain in lockdown for three years. A name for this scenario could be 'The Bankruptcy Era.'

The fifth is a Different but Much Better Scenario. For example, the virus gets eradicated in the developed world within nine months, and a breakthrough vaccine saves the developing world within eighteen months. A name for this scenario could be 'The Wake-up Call.'

Once you have developed these five scenarios for your industry (via discussions with experts in several fields), you can keep all five scenarios alive in the minds of your leaders and move quickly when one of these scenarios begins to eventuate. Many businesses hoped for The Kangaroo Bounce or The Wake-up Call scenarios to play out. Yet approaching business strategy without telling stories like The L-Shaped Road to Recovery or The Bankruptcy Era is foolish.

Jeff, my local gym owner sold his highly successful business to a large corporate chain for a nice profit in late 2019. After ten years in business, he sold at a great time. In 2020, all around the world, dozens of airlines and thousands of fitness centres, restaurants, cafes, night clubs, taxi companies and event venues, went bankrupt.

As a result of production cuts by OPEC, oil prices crashed and then skyrocketed. Many universities and some private schools failed. Thousands of manufacturing and retail businesses closed their factories and stores. Some forever.

On the other hand, Coronavirus was an economic dream-come-true for businesses in online gambling, home improvement, food delivery, online retail and movie streaming subscriptions. Pet and pet care product sales went through the roof, along with alcohol and tobacco sales. Opportunity and crisis came together in stark relief. Has the crisis of the early 2020s hurt or helped your business? Have you had to move your business online? Perhaps sooner than previously planned. Going digital has been a necessity, rather than an option for millions of businesses. If Coronavirus has destroyed the industry you once worked in and you are not sure what might happen next, consider using scenario planning.

It's time to make some notes on the pages that follow. What alternatives and options exist for your business with each scenario? Scenario planning does not require you to chase two or more futures and build capabilities for each in anticipation. Scenario planning helps you create options, navigate uncertainty and act sooner.

Jot down your five scenarios.

APPENDIX E: SCENARIO PLANNING

1. OFFICAL FUTURE 'STATUS QUO'

2. SAME BUT WORSE	3. SAME BUT BETTER
'LONGER ROAD'	'KANGAROO BOUNCE'
4. DIFFERENT BUT WORSE	**5. DIFFERENT BUT BETTER**
'BANKRUPTCY ERA'	'WAKEUP CALL'

1. OFFICAL FUTURE 'STATUS QUO'

2. SAME BUT WORSE	3. SAME BUT BETTER
4. DIFFERENT BUT WORSE	**5. DIFFERENT BUT BETTER**

"It is always worth asking yourself: how could I be wrong?"

Peter Schwartz

APPENDIX F

DECISION TREES

A tool to help answer 'what if' questions is a Decision Tree. A Decision Tree is a diagram that compares options.

Imagine you are an Australian livestock farmer who owns 5000 grass-fed cattle in north-western New South Wales, near the rural township of Casino. Imagine also, that you own your farm outright and that farms around Casino sell for $3M.

At the moment, the market price for cattle is $1000 per head.

Let's pretend you have new neighbours, Donald and Jacinda who live on adjacent farms. They too have 5000 head of cattle and have both purchased their farms for around $3M each. Earlier today on your verandah, you shared a glass of tea with Donald and Jacinda and discussed the longer-term weather outlook. Donald grew up in Oklahoma cattle country and had recently moved to Australia. Jacinda had also arrived recently, having grown up on a dairy farm in New Zealand.

THE STRATEGY NOTE

Donald moved to Australia during the recent floods and has seen nothing but green pastures. Donald's scenario for longer-term weather is continuing wet seasons and plenty of grass. Jacinda remembers Australia's recent multi-year drought and the previous season's bushfires. Jacinda believes that Climate Change means more dry spells, with fewer wet seasons. On hearing Jacinda speak, Donald, an arrogant climate sceptic, laughs at her ideas.

Donald is convinced that good wet weather is ahead. He shares that his bank has just approved a loan of three million dollars, which he will use to buy a further 3000 cattle. Jacinda sees Donald's move as risky and decides that she will simply hold onto the 5000 cattle she has.

When pressed by Donald and Jacinda, you point out that it is essential to consider the full range of scenarios such as; floods, multi-year droughts, wet seasons and dry spells. After exploring scenarios with Donald and Jacinda, you do some research on the internet. YouTube interviews with climate scientists and regional elders point to more droughts in the near future.

What should you do?

When it floods, farmers in your region often lose 50% of their herd to drownings and disease.

During a wet season, healthy cattle are worth $1500, not $1000.

During a dry spell, cattle demand jumps and the head price increases from $1000 to $1200.

APPENDIX F: DECISION TREES

In a drought, cattle lose weight quickly and additional food needs to be purchased for the cattle.

The next step is to give each of your four scenarios names along with descriptions. These names could be 'Floods, Wet Seasons, Dry Spells and Droughts.'

Based on your research, you assign probabilities to each of these scenarios.

Probability of Floods over the next two years = 10%
Probability of Wet Seasons over the next two years = 10%
Probability of Dry Spells over the next two years = 20%
Probability of Droughts over the next two years = 60%

As a livestock farmer using a Decision Tree, you have captured four scenarios and their probabilities.

Finally, you name possible options.

Plan A. Buy 3000 cattle.
Plan B. Hold onto the 5000 cattle you have.
Plan C. Sell 3000 cattle to Donald.

Which is the best strategy?

Plan A, Plan B or Plan C?

THE STRATEGY NOTE

The Decision Tree on the following page offers a visual representation of these options.

On the pages that follow, create a Decision Tree for your own business using a range of scenarios, their probabilities and the options you are considering for your business.

APPENDIX F: DECISION TREES

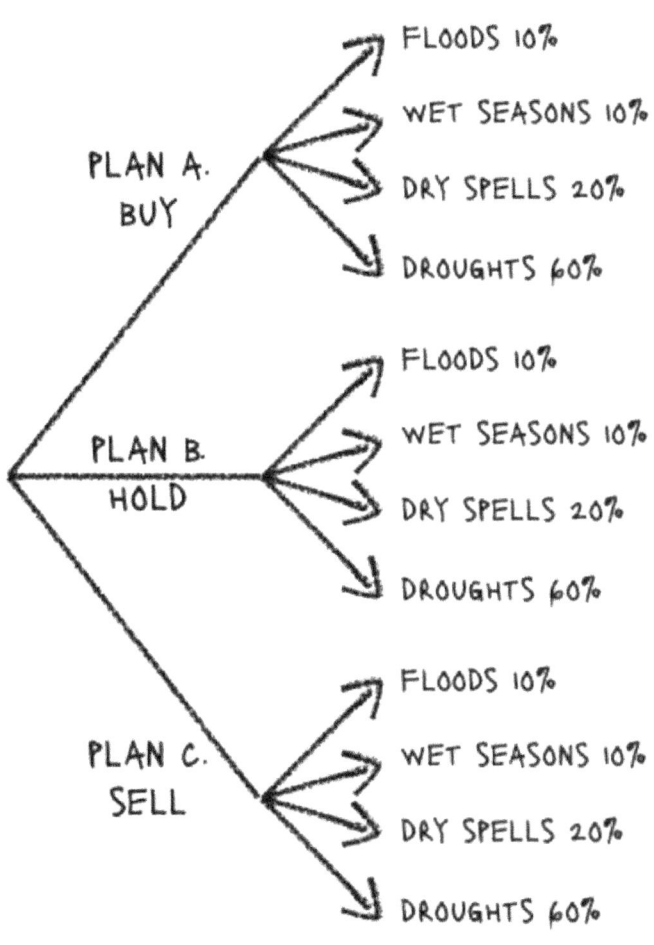

"The possible solutions to a given problem emerge as the leaves of a tree, each node representing a point of deliberation and decision."

Niklaus Wirth

APPENDIX G

EXPECTED MONETARY VALUES

Once you have created a Decision Tree with your options, scenarios and the probabilities of those scenarios, you can carry out Expected Monetary Value (EMV) calculations to find your best option (Plan A, Plan B or Plan C).

The EMV is the sum of each [scenario payoff x that scenario's probability].

For example, the EMV of cattle in two-years, taking into account all scenarios can be calculated this way.

The 10% Flood Scenario, where 0.5 or 50% of cattle survive = 0.1 x $1000 x 0.5 = $50 per head

THE STRATEGY NOTE

The 10% Wet Season Scenario, where the price goes to $1500 = 0.1 x $1500 = $150 per head

The 20% Dry Spell Scenario, where the price goes to $1200 = 0.2 x $1200 = $240 per head

The 60% Drought Scenario, where the price goes to $400 = 0.6 x $400 = $240 per head

So, the EMV for cattle, taking into account all four scenarios is:

EMV = Sum ($50 + $150 + $240 + $240) = $680 per head

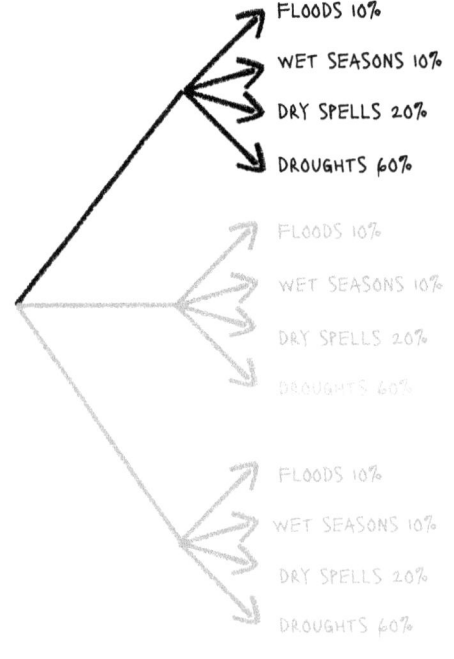

APPENDIX G: EXPECTED MONETARY VALUES

The EMV of $680 tells us that on average we might expect the value of cattle to fall from $1000 per head to $680 in the coming two years. At this point, I might add that in the real-world, proper sensitivity analysis of the allocated probabilities often leads to less stable predictions. For this example, small shifts in weather can upset the assigned probabilities, distort results and provide riskier conclusions.

Let's assume Donald decides to mortgage 100% of his farm to buy 3000 cattle. He will soon have 8000 cattle. From our EMV calculations we expect the value of Donald's 8000 cattle to fall from $8M to $5.44M.

Because Jacinda has decided to neither buy or sell, we expect the value of her 5000 cattle to fall from $5M to $3.4M over the next two years

As an options focused livestock farmer, you have created a Decision Tree that includes all four scenarios and the probabilities of those scenarios. Your EMV calculations help you to decide what action to take. As you expect the value of your 5000 cattle to drop to $3.4M, you decide to promptly sell 3000 of your cattle to Donald at $1000 per head, netting you $3M.

While you understand that a Decision Tree is a helpful tool, there may be other factors at work you have not taken into account. You decide to use your Decision Tree as a guide, but not an absolute truth. You also remember that people, including yourself, are terrible at listening to scenarios about a disaster. A terrible event somewhere else in the world could raise the price of cattle, even during a drought. For example, in an unforeseen global pandemic, massive food shortages in China or the US could be beneficial to your business!

You find a way to hedge your bets. You offer Donald an option contract that allows him to buy your remaining 2000 cattle in a year for $2.4M, if Donald pays you $0.2M today for that right. Donald loves what he thinks is a good deal. He accepts your offer, which gives him the right, but not the obligation to acquire your 2000 remaining cattle in 12 months for $2.4M or $1200 per head.

Selling this option to Donald gives you a further $0.2M.

You then lease your unused pastures to Donald over the next two years for an upfront payment of $0.3M.

Now, imagine being two drought-filled years down the road. Since you took the time to consider scenarios, their probabilities and calculated expected monetary values, are you in a better position than Donald and Jacinda?

Two years ago, Donald, Jacinda and you each had a net worth of $8M, comprising a $3M farm and $5M worth of livestock.

You still own your farm = $3M, and you have $3M from the sale of 3000 cattle to Donald. You have an option premium from Donald = $0.2M. You have lease income from Donald = $0.3M. And you still own 2000 cattle, that after twelve months, Donald wisely chose not to buy. Your cattle are worth $1.12M.

APPENDIX G: EXPECTED MONETARY VALUES

After two years, your net worth becomes $7.86M.

By contrast, Jacinda still owns her farm = $3M, and 5000 cattle that are worth $3.4M.

Jacinda's net worth is $6.4M.

Alas, Donald's bank owns his farm. Donald paid you $0.5M for an option premium and lease payment, and he now owns 8000 underweight cattle worth around $5.44M.

Donald's net worth is now $4.94M.

Naming your options, building scenarios, drawing decision trees, assigning probability and calculating EMVs will not guarantee that your business always makes a profit. However, it will help you to avoid making catastrophic errors that result in huge losses.

On the pages that follow, if applicable, carry out Expected Monetary Value (EMV) calculations to help find the best options for your business.

When you use an EMV calculation to reach a particular decision, revisit your assumptions. Even if that decision has a majority of support from your people, it will be helpful to pause and reflect. What other factors have not been taken into account in your calculations. For example, have you accounted for environmental and ethical factors? In terms of human health and sustainable global food production

The scenario of healthy vegetable-based superfoods replacing traditional meat sources is likely to occur over the next decade. Such decisions might be triggered by our experiences with climate change, greater awareness of animal suffering or viral loads in meat factories and advancing knowledge of the links between domestic meat consumption, heart disease and cancer. When these factors are also considered, the farming and harvesting of meat may become less palatable. And, in turn, less profitable.

APPENDIX G: EXPECTED MONETARY VALUES

"Whenever you find yourself on the side of the majority, it is time to pause and reflect."

Mark Twain

ENDNOTES

INTRODUCTION

[1] Bhikkhu Bodhi (1999). *The Noble Eightfold Path: The Way to the End of Suffering.*

[2] Myriam Sidibe. *Marketing Meets Mission. Learning from brands that have taken on global health challenges.* Harvard Business Review May 2020.

[3] William Yost (Bill) passed away peacefully on 29 October 2019. As an Adjunct Professor at The Anderson School of Management at UCLA, Bill was named Outstanding Teacher of the Year seven times, and Businessweek named him one of the Best Professors of Entrepreneurship in the USA.

[4] Jim Collins (2001). *Good to Great: Why Some Companies Make the Leap and Others Don't.* William Collins.

[5] Walter Isaacson. *The Real Leadership Lessons of Steve Jobs.* Harvard Business Review April 2012.

[6] Olivia Solon. '*Uber fired more than 20 employees after a company investigation into sexual harassment claims and workplace culture.*' The Guardian on 7 June 2017.

TASK ONE - WRITE YOUR RECOMMENDATION

7 T.J. Rodgers. *No Excuses Management.* Harvard Business Reveiw, July 1990.

8 Martin Seligman (1972). *Learned helplessness.* Annual Review of Medicine. 23 (1): 407–412.

9 On Friday, 24 April 2020, 23-year-old John Mondello tragically committed suicide after working less than three months as an Emergency Medical Technician (EMT) with the Fire Department of New York (FDNY). Just two days later, on Sunday, 26 April 2020, Dr. Lorna Breen, a 49-year-old ER doctor at New York Presbyterian Allen Hospital, took her own life. New York Daily News. 27 April 2020.

TASK TWO – REPORT YOUR HEALTH

10 Leander Kahney (2019). *Tim Cook: The Genius Who Took Apple to the Next Level.* Penguin Books Ltd.

11 Oleg Petrenko et al. *The Case for Humble Expectations: CEO Humility and Market Performance.* Strategic Management Journal, 2019.

12 Jim Collins (2001). *Good to Great: Why Some Companies Make the Leap and Others Don't.* William Collins.

13 Justin Bariso. *Uber's CEO Just Taught a Powerful Lesson in Emotional Intelligence. Here it is in 5 Word*s. Inc Magazine December 2018.

14 Lauren Eskreis-Winkler. *Maybe Failure Isn't the Best Teacher.* Harvard Business Review, May 2020.

15 Carol Dweck (2006). *Mindset: Changing the Way You Think to Fulfil Your Potential.* Brown Book Group.

16 Walter Isaacson. *The Real Leadership Lessons of Steve Jobs.* Harvard Business Review, April 2012.

ENDNOTES

TASK THREE – SUMMARIZE YOUR ANALYSIS

[17] Jim Collins and Jerry Porras (1994). *Built to Last: Successful Habits of Visionary Companies.* Harper Business.

[18] Frederick Allen (1994). *Secret Formula: The Inside Story of How Coca-Cola Became the Best-Known Brand in the World.* Harper Paperbacks.

[19] John Hale (2020). *The Strategy Book: Create a Strategic Mindset and Future-Proof your Business.* Hale Consulting Group.

[20] Joseph Campbell (1990). *The Hero's Journey: Joseph Campbell on His Life and Work.* New World Library.

TASK FOUR – NAME YOUR OPTIONS

[21] Bill Gates. *The next outbreak? We are not ready.* TED 2015.

[22] *Wuhan in Coronavirus Lockdown: Stories of Courage and Determination.* Makalu Publication House. www.china.org.cn

TASK FIVE – GROW DIGITAL WINGS

[23] Timothy Brook; Jerome Bourgon; Gregory Blue (2008). *Death by a Thousand Cuts.* Harvard University Press.

[24] Peter Weill and Stephanie Woerner (2018). *What's Your Digital Business Model?* Harvard Business Review Press.

[25] Michael Kanaan (2020). *T-Minus AI: Humanity's Countdown to Artificial Intelligence and the New Pursuit of Global Power.* Ben Bella Books.

[26] Amy Webb (2016). *The Signals Are Talking: Why Today's Fringe Is Tomorrow's Mainstream.* Hachette Book Group NY.

[27] Peter Weill; Thomas Apel; Stephanie Woerner and Jennifer Banner. *It Pays to Have a Digitally Savy Board.* MIT Sloan Management Review. March 2019.

28. Michael Becraft (2014). *Bill Gates: A Biography.* Greenwood Biographies.
29. Roger Martin. *What Managers Get Wrong About Capital.* Harvard Business Review, May 2020.
30. Rita McGrath and Ryan McManus. *Discovery-Driven Digital Transformation.* HBR, May 2020.

TASK SIX – ALIGN YOUR ACTIONS
31. Dave Carroll (2012). *United Breaks Guitars: The Power of One Voice in the Age of Social Media.* Hay House Inc.
32. Sonsofmaxwell YouTube (2009). *United Break Guitars.*
33. David Dao (2020). *Dragged Off.*
34. Joey Coleman (2018). *Never Lose a Customer Again: Turn Any Sale into Lifelong Loyalty in 100 Days.* Portfolio Penguin.

CONCLUSION
35. Mike Isaac (2019). *Super Pumped: The Battle for Uber.* W.W. Norton & Company Ltd, NY.

APPENDIX A. INDUSTRY ATTRACTIVENESS
36. Joan Magretta (2012). *Understanding Michael Porter: The Essential Guide to Competition and Strategy.* Harvard Business School Press.

APPENDIX B. CLAIM TO FAME
37. Robert Macklin and Peter Thompson (2010). *The Big Fella: The Rise and Rise of BHP Billiton.* Griffin Press Australia.

ENDNOTES

APPENDIX C. CRITICAL SUCCESS FACTORS

[38] Neville Isdell and David Beasley (2012). *Inside Coca-Cola: A CEO's Life Story of Building the World's Most Popular Brand.* St. Martin's Griffin.

APPENDIX D. CUSTOMER INTIMACY WHEEL

[39] Walter Isaacson. *The Real Leadership Lessons of Steve Jobs.* Harvard Business Review, April 2012.
[40] Leander Kahney (2008). *Inside Steve's Brain.* Atlantic Books, London.
[41] Robert Bruce (2000). *Creating Your Strategic Future.* Harper Collins.

APPENDIX E. SCENARIO PLANNING

[42] Peter Schwartz (1991). *The Art of the Long View: Planning for the Future in an Uncertain World.* Doubleday NY.

ACKNOWLEDGEMENTS

I have learned a great deal about the art of implementing strategy from many quarters. When it comes to the inspiration for *The Strategy Note*, I would like to acknowledge the thought leadership of Harvard Business School, Melbourne Business School, Virginia Lewis, Renée Mauborgne, Amy Webb, Robert Bruce, W. Chan Kim, Neil Churchill, Jim Collins, Oscar Hauptman, Michael Porter, T.J. Rogers, Richard Rumelt, Peter Schwartz and Peter Weill. In memory, I am thankful to Bill Yost, who taught leaders across the planet the secrets to growing businesses successfully.

I am thankful to colleagues, friends and family for their willingness to read early drafts of *The Strategy Note* and offer generous feedback: Fran Ackerman, Valentin Aoudai, Robert Bruce, James Carlopio, Dolores Cummins, Marion Farrelly, Ian Gilbert, Rowan Gilmore, Jan Hale, Rebecca Hale, Oscar Hauptman, Natasha Milne, Brad Reece, Tom Smith, Bryan Worn and Peter Yates. I am grateful to my talented daughter Lauren Hale, for creating the illustrations for this book. Finally, I would like to thank my wife, Johanna. Birthing a book and nurturing an author, requires patience and love. Without Johanna's devotion, neither would exist.

ABOUT THE AUTHOR

John Hale is the founder of Hale Consulting Group, a globally focused management consulting firm specializing in strategy, people and change. As a keynote speaker, John has delivered over a thousand talks in twelve countries across four continents, to leaders from Fortune 500 and mid-sized companies to start-ups and public sector organizations. John has also worked as an early stage investor and advisor. He has been a Visiting and Adjunct Professor and has taught at various institutions, including Singapore Management University, Bond University and Melbourne Business School.

As a young child, John grew up in the developed and developing world. Living in both patriarchal and matrilineal cultures grounded him in the need for truth and justice as well as the ethics of care and co-operation. John brings a balance of sense and sensibility to his work. He currently resides in Australia.

Hale Consulting Group is dedicated to helping organizations of all kinds drive value through better strategy, leadership and corporate wellbeing.

Please visit our website and explore

Keynote Speaking: John Hale shares value-driven ideas and strategies with thousands of leaders each year at global forums, national conferences and company events.

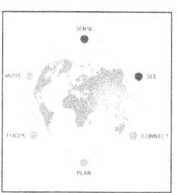

Consulting: HCG Consultants deliver strategy and organizational assignments for corporate, industry and professional groups, across a variety of industries in various parts of the globe.

Leadership Mentoring: HCG Consultants provide expert mentoring programs that empower leaders and help organizations advance in healthy ways.

www.halecg.com +61 407 301 200

www.ingramcontent.com/pod-product-compliance
Lightning Source LLC
Chambersburg PA
CBHW070254010526
44107CB00056B/2454